The Dreamer Premium

How to Think, Work, and Thrive in the Age of AI

Brian R. Miller

2026

Contents

The Dreamer Premium

The Dreamer Premium

How to Think, Work, and Thrive in the Age of AI

Brian R. Miller

SYNTHETIC INSIGHTS PUBLISHING

First Edition · 2026

Published by Synthetic Insights Publishing

ISBN: 979-8-9946737-6-8 (Paperback)
ISBN: 979-8-9946737-5-1 (eBook)

Companion resources:
https://synthetic-insights.ai/the-dreamer-premium

Printed in the United States of America

First Edition

How to Think, Work, and Thrive in the Age of AI

By Brian R. Miller

SYNTHETIC INSIGHTS PUBLISHING

First Edition - 2026

Published by Synthetic Insights Publishing

ISBN: 979-8-9946737-6-8 (Paperback) ISBN: 979-8-9946737-5-1 (eBook)

Companion resources: https://synthetic-insights.ai/the-dreamer-premium

---

About This Book

This book is written for anyone who wants to understand AI well enough to use it effectively—without needing a technical background. Whether you're a business professional, manager, knowledge worker, or simply curious about AI's role in work and life, this guide provides practical wisdom for navigating the AI age.

The approach is grounded in real experience: the author has spent years working with AI tools across professional contexts, from enterprise security to software development. What you'll find here isn't theoretical speculation but tested patterns that work.

Who This Book Is For

Business Professionals – If you want to understand AI capabilities and limitations for strategic decisions, start with Part 1 and work through sequentially.

Managers and Executives – Focus on Part 4 (Implications) for workforce and organizational considerations. Part 5 offers ethical frameworks for leadership.

Knowledge Workers – Part 3 (AI in Practice) gives you immediately applicable patterns for writing, research, decision-making, and productivity.

Ethically-Minded Readers – Part 5 explores ethics and values in depth, including perspectives from multiple wisdom traditions.

General Readers – Read straight through. The book builds understanding progressively from foundations to practice to implications to ethics.

How to Use This Book

This book uses several content types:

- **Main Text** – Core concepts for all readers
- **"Try This" Boxes** – Simple exercises you can do immediately
- **"Think About It" Boxes** – Reflection prompts for deeper engagement
- **"Key Point" Callouts** – Essential concepts to remember

Read the main text for understanding. Use the boxes based on your interests and how deeply you want to engage.

Acknowledgments

This book emerges from years of working with AI across professional and personal contexts. I'm grateful to everyone who made it possible.

To the AI research community – for building tools that genuinely augment human capability while taking safety seriously.

To my colleagues and collaborators – for countless conversations about AI's role in work and life that shaped the thinking in this book.

To the readers of "Agentic Development" – whose feedback on the technical book inspired this companion volume for general audiences.

To my family – for patience with the late nights of writing and for asking the practical questions that kept this book grounded.

For everyone navigating work and life in an AI-augmented world.

About the Author

Brian R. Miller is Chief Information Security Officer at Healthfirst, New York's largest nonprofit health insurer. Recognized as a Top 100 CISO, Brian brings over 25 years of experience spanning government, defense, and healthcare sectors to his exploration of AI's role in professional and personal life.

A pioneer in AI-driven automation since 2016, Brian previously spent 13 years at Booz Allen Hamilton advising the Department of Defense, NSA, NIST, and federal intelligence agencies. He serves on venture capital advisory boards for Viola Ventures and Glilot Capital Partners.

Brian holds an Executive Certificate in Public Policy from Harvard Kennedy School, an MS from Johns Hopkins University, and an MA in Global Leadership from Fuller Theological Seminary. This diverse background—spanning technology, business, and theology—directly shapes the multidisciplinary approach of this book.

Connect with Brian: https://linkedin.com/in/brian-r-miller-ciso

---

First Edition Published 2026

Synthetic Insights Publishing

CONTENTS

Part 4: Implications

Part 5: Ethics and Human Flourishing

Back Matter

Preface: The AI Moment We're In

I hadn't written code since the 1980s. I remembered BASIC, vaguely. The thought of building software seemed as distant as my college programming courses.

Then, in June 2025, I sat down with an AI assistant and described an application I wanted to build. Three hours later, I had a working prototype. By the end of the day, it was deployed to the cloud with authentication, a database, and an automated deployment process I barely understood.

I stared at the screen, genuinely unsettled. Not because the AI had done something magical—but because the barrier I'd assumed existed between "people who can build software" and "everyone else" had simply... dissolved.

That was my AI moment. The moment I realized something fundamental had shifted.

Something changed around 2023—not just the technology, but what became possible for people like me. AI systems that could hold conversations, write coherently, and reason through problems went from research projects to products anyone could use. Millions of people who'd never thought about AI started using it daily. Organizations that had been talking about AI for years suddenly had it on their doorstep—

ready or not.

We're living in the aftermath of that shift. AI isn't coming; it's here. The question isn't whether to engage with it—it's how.

Why This Moment Is Different

People have been predicting AI revolutions for decades. So what makes this time different?

Capability crossed a threshold. Previous AI systems could do impressive things in narrow domains—play chess, recognize faces, recommend products. Current systems can engage with language itself—reading, writing, reasoning, conversing across virtually any domain. That generality changes everything.

Accessibility changed. You no longer need technical expertise to use AI. Conversational interfaces put AI capability within reach of anyone who can type a sentence. The barrier to entry dropped to nearly zero.

Speed surprised everyone. The pace of improvement caught even experts off guard. Capabilities that seemed years away arrived in months. No one knows with confidence what AI will be able to do in five years—including the people building it.

Integration accelerated. AI is becoming embedded in the tools you already use—word processors, email, search, design software. You may be using AI without realizing it.

What's at Stake

This moment matters because decisions being made now—by individuals, organizations, and societies—will shape how AI develops and how it affects us.

For you personally: How you engage with AI shapes your career, your productivity, and your relationship with technology. Those who understand AI and use it well gain real advantages. Those who ignore it risk being left behind—not because AI replaces them, but because people who use AI well outpace them.

For organizations: AI adoption isn't optional—your competitors are adopting it. The question is whether you adopt thoughtfully, with appropriate governance, or chaotically, with uncontrolled risks.

For all of us: How AI is developed and deployed affects everyone—through its impact on jobs, truth, privacy, creativity, and more. The choices being made now will echo for decades.

The Challenge of This Moment

Here's the challenge: understanding hasn't kept pace with capability.

Most people using AI don't really understand what it is or how it works. They don't know its genuine capabilities or its genuine limitations. They can't distinguish what AI does well from what it does poorly. They don't know how to use it effectively—or how to use it responsibly.

That gap creates problems:

- People over-trust AI and get burned by confident errors
- People under-use AI and miss genuine opportunities
- People use AI in ways that create ethical problems they didn't anticipate
- Organizations adopt AI without appropriate governance
- Individuals worry about AI affecting their careers without knowing how to respond

Closing this gap is urgent. Not because AI is dangerous and must be stopped, but because AI is powerful and needs to be understood.

A Path Forward

This book offers one path through the current moment.

It begins with honest understanding—what AI actually is, what it can and can't do, how to think about its capabilities and limitations.

It builds practical skill—how to work with AI effectively, how to provide context, how to communicate productively.

It applies these to real domains—writing, research, decision-making, productivity.

It addresses the bigger picture—workforce changes, organizational challenges, career implications.

And it engages with the deeper questions—ethics, values, what it means to live well with AI.

My goal isn't to predict AI's future or tell you exactly what to think about it. It's to help you navigate this moment with understanding, skill, and wisdom.

The AI moment we're in is genuinely new. But human beings have navigated technological transitions before. We can do it again—if we approach this one with clear eyes and thoughtful intention.

That's what this book is for. Let's begin.

January 2026

Introduction

Why This Book

In two years, AI went from novelty to necessity.

In 2023, ChatGPT was a curiosity—a clever party trick you showed friends, an interesting experiment you played with occasionally. By 2026, AI tools have become woven into how millions of people work, learn, create, and think.

But adoption has outpaced understanding.

People use AI daily without knowing what it actually is or how it works. They worry about AI taking their jobs while missing opportunities to make their work better. They fear AI's risks while failing to use it responsibly. They either over-rely on AI as an oracle or dismiss it as hype—neither approach serving them well.

This book exists to close that gap.

I wrote this for people who want to understand AI well enough to use it wisely—not as technologists, but as thoughtful humans navigating a changing world. Whether you're using AI for work, creativity, learning, or everyday life, this book offers practical guidance grounded in honest understanding.

What You'll Find Here

The book moves from understanding to practice to implication to wisdom—five parts that build on each other but can also be read independently. If you're not sure where to start, the "Who This Book Is For" section in the front matter offers a quick routing guide based on your background and interests.

My Journey With AI

I came to AI as a practitioner, not a researcher.

As a technology leader responsible for cybersecurity, I watched AI tools transform how my teams worked. In security operations, we went from drowning in hundreds of thousands of alerts to processing them automatically, with only a fraction needing human attention. I saw what AI could do when thoughtfully applied—and what could go wrong when it wasn't.

I also came as a learner. As I describe in the Preface, discovering AI coding assistants demolished barriers I'd assumed were permanent. That experience taught me something I keep returning to throughout this book: AI amplifies capability regardless of your starting point, but wisdom about how to use it doesn't come automatically. Wisdom requires understanding—and that's what this book provides.

This book draws on that practical experience—real use of AI in real work, real mistakes made and lessons learned, real thinking about what this technology means for how we work and live.

What You Won't Find Here

This book won't make you an AI engineer. If you want to understand how to build AI systems, look elsewhere.

It won't predict the future. AI is developing rapidly, and specific predictions quickly become obsolete. Instead, I focus on principles that remain relevant as capabilities evolve.

It won't tell you exactly what to do. I offer frameworks for thinking, not prescriptions for acting.

It won't pretend AI is simple. AI involves genuine complexity, real limitations, and hard tradeoffs. I try to present these honestly rather than oversimplifying.

And it won't hype AI or dismiss it. AI is genuinely capable and genuinely limited. Understanding both is where useful guidance begins.

An Invitation

Technology that seemed like science fiction has become daily reality. This creates both opportunity and responsibility.

The opportunity: to accomplish more, learn faster, create better, work smarter. AI genuinely enables things that weren't possible before.

The responsibility: to use this capability wisely, ethically, and in service of human flourishing. Technology amplifies human intentions—whether those intentions are good or ill.

This book is an invitation to engage with AI thoughtfully. Not to fear it or worship it, but to understand it well enough to use it well. To be neither uncritical adopter nor stubborn resister, but a thoughtful practitioner who makes deliberate choices about how to work with AI.

The future isn't determined by technology. It's determined by human choices about how to use technology. Those choices start with understanding.

That understanding starts now.

Chapter 1: What AI Actually Is (And Isn't)

When my team at a major healthcare company faced 600,000 security incidents in a single year, we had a choice: hire over 200 analysts or find a different approach. We chose AI. Today, six analysts handle that same volume—not by working harder, but by working with AI systems that never sleep, never get distracted, and process patterns across millions of data points in seconds.

Here's what I've learned from that experience: understanding what AI actually *is* matters more than understanding what it can *do*. When you understand the nature of these systems, you stop being impressed by the magic show and start seeing how to make them genuinely useful in your life.

CHAPTER OVERVIEW

What you'll learn: - How AI actually works (no technical background required) - The real capabilities and limitations of today's AI - Common misconceptions that lead people astray - How to think clearly about AI claims and hype

Why it matters: Clear understanding prevents both over-reliance and missed opportunities.

Reading time: About 15 minutes

The Pattern Recognition Machine

Here's a mental model that will serve you well: AI is pattern recognition at scale.

That's it. Not consciousness. Not thinking. Not understanding in the way you and I understand things. Modern AI systems—the ones you interact with through ChatGPT, Claude, or the AI assistant on your phone—work by finding patterns in enormous amounts of data and then using those patterns to generate responses.

Imagine you've read every book, article, and conversation ever written in English. You haven't *understood* any of it in the way a human would, but you've noticed patterns. You know that when someone says "The capital of France is..." the next word is almost always "Paris." You know that professional emails tend to follow certain structures. You know that when people describe symptoms, certain diagnoses tend to follow.

That's roughly what a **large language model** (or LLM) does. It's been trained on vast amounts of text—books, websites, code, conversations—and it has learned the patterns of how words, ideas, and concepts relate to each other. When you ask it a question, it generates a response by predicting what words should come next, based on all those patterns it has learned.

This might sound less impressive than "artificial intelligence," but understanding it makes you a better user of these tools. You stop expecting the AI to "just know" things you haven't told it. You start providing the context it needs. You learn to verify its outputs where accuracy matters.

> **KEY POINT**
>
> AI doesn't "know" things the way you know your own phone number. It recognizes patterns. This distinction helps you understand both its remarkable capabilities and its surprising blind spots.

What AI Can Do Today

Here's what AI can actually accomplish—because the gap between marketing claims and reality can be wide.

AI excels at:

Processing and synthesizing information. Ask an AI to summarize a long document, and it extracts key points with impressive accuracy. Need to understand a complex topic quickly? AI can give you a clear overview in seconds. When I'm preparing for a board presentation, I use AI to synthesize research from dozens of sources into coherent narratives. What used to take days now takes hours.

Generating first drafts. Writing from a blank page is hard. AI can give you a starting point—a draft email, a report structure, a list of options to consider. You'll almost always need to revise, but starting from something is easier than starting from nothing.

Finding patterns humans miss. AI can analyze data across dimensions that would take humans months or years to process. In security, AI systems spot attack patterns by correlating events across thousands of endpoints simultaneously. In business, AI can identify trends in customer behavior that no human analyst would have time to discover.

Explaining and teaching. Want to understand how a complex system works? AI can explain it at whatever level of detail you need, adjusting its explanation based on your follow-up questions. This makes AI a surprisingly good tutor and thought partner.

Automating routine tasks. Anything that follows predictable patterns—formatting documents, categorizing information, generating standard responses—AI can handle with high reliability.

> **TRY THIS**
>
> Think of something you need to explain to someone else—a project, a decision, a concept. Ask an AI assistant to help you explain it at three different levels: for a complete begin-

ner, for someone with moderate knowledge, and for an expert. Notice how the AI adapts its language and emphasis. This skill of adjusting explanations is something AI does remarkably well.

What AI Cannot Do

Here's where things get interesting—and where understanding the pattern-recognition nature of AI really pays off.

AI cannot reason about novel situations the way humans can. AI excels at pattern matching, not at stepping back and asking, "Wait, does this actually make sense?" When confronted with unfamiliar problems—situations that don't match its training data—AI often produces confidently wrong answers. Newer models are getting better at textbook logic puzzles, but the core limitation remains: recognizing patterns and genuinely reasoning through something new are different cognitive acts.

AI cannot provide meaning or purpose. This might sound abstract, but it matters enormously. I learned this firsthand while exploring a study I'd come across in graduate school—one that showed a strong statistical correlation between the number of storks in a region and the number of babies born there. I asked an AI to analyze the relationship, curious what it would make of an obviously spurious correlation.

The AI hedged. It said the correlation "might be causal, might be coincidental," and suggested several mechanisms by which storks could theoretically be associated with birth rates—nesting patterns near hospitals, shared environmental factors, population density effects. It treated the question as a genuine statistical puzzle.

As a human being, I could tell you in two seconds: storks don't bring babies. I didn't need to run a regression or consult a dataset. I have *meaning*—a commonsense understanding of how the world works, of what causes what, of what's absurd even when the numbers line up. AI doesn't have that. It can find the pattern. It cannot tell you the pattern is nonsense.

AI can tell you *what* is efficient, but not *why* efficiency should be your goal. It can analyze options, but it cannot tell you what you should value. Philosophers and theologians have wrestled with questions of meaning for millennia—questions that pattern recognition cannot touch. Meaning—the sense that your work matters, that your life has purpose, that some things are worth pursuing regardless of measurable outcomes—remains distinctly human.

AI cannot maintain genuine understanding across contexts. When you start a conversation with an AI, it typically has no memory of your previous conversations. Every interaction starts fresh. The AI might seem to "know" you during a conversation, but it's simply tracking patterns within that single session. This is why the same AI can give you contradictory advice on different days—it's not remembering and learning; it's just pattern-matching in each moment.

AI cannot verify its own outputs. This is the limitation that catches people most off guard. When AI generates text that sounds confident and authoritative, it has no way to check whether what it's saying is actually true. It generates plausible-sounding text, but "plausible-sounding" and "true" are not the same thing. This is why AI sometimes "hallucinates"—producing confident-sounding nonsense that fits the patterns it learned but doesn't match reality. You'll see a vivid example of this in the "Common Misconceptions" section below—a hallucination that looked perfectly polished until I checked it against what actually happened.

THINK ABOUT IT

Think about a decision you made recently that involved weighing values—not just calculating optimal outcomes, but deciding what actually mattered to you. How would AI have approached that decision differently? What would have been lost if you'd delegated it entirely to a pattern-recognition system?

The Gap Between Hype and Reality

Every few months, breathless headlines announce that AI is about to transform everything—that millions of jobs will disappear overnight, that AI will soon outthink humans at everything, that we're on the verge of artificial general intelligence.

Here's a more grounded perspective, based on what I've seen in actual organizations.

The job transformation story. Goldman Sachs research (Briggs & Kodnani, 2023) estimated that about 7% of US employment could face displacement from generative AI—but that most affected jobs would be *complemented* rather than *replaced*, and that AI could boost global GDP by 7% over a decade. As of early 2026, the Yale Budget Lab's ongoing labor market analysis has found no correlation between a job's AI exposure and unemployment changes. What's happening isn't mass job elimination—it's job *transformation*. My security team didn't shrink because of AI; their work transformed from repetitive alert-triage to strategic threat hunting and security architecture.

The "thinking" illusion. When you interact with a sophisticated AI, it feels like you're talking to something that understands. The conversational fluency is remarkable. But the appearance of understanding is not the same as understanding. Meaning and critical thinking remain human domains—no matter how convincing the simulation becomes.

The timeline question. Predictions about when AI will achieve various milestones have consistently been wrong—sometimes by overestimating, sometimes by underestimating. What I can tell you is that the AI you can use today is genuinely useful for many tasks, and that's worth more than speculation about what AI might be able to do in ten years.

The right stance isn't fear or hype—it's clear-eyed assessment. What matters is understanding AI well enough to use it effectively and to protect the value you bring as a human thinker.

Common Misconceptions

Here are some beliefs that trip people up:

"AI understands what I mean." No, AI processes what you say. The difference matters. If you ask for "a good restaurant nearby," AI doesn't understand your preferences, your budget, or what "good" means to you—unless you've told it. This is why learning to provide context (which we'll cover in later chapters) dramatically improves your results.

"If AI sounds confident, it must be right." I learned this one the hard way. While writing a book, I asked AI to consolidate my notes from a multi-day professional development class—pulling together speakers, topics, and key takeaways into a coherent summary. What I got back looked clean and well-organized. The writing was polished. It read like a perfectly reasonable account.

Except it wasn't. The AI had taken a speaker from the first day of the class and associated their remarks with the last day. On the surface, this looked like nothing—just a different date attached to the same content. But it changed the meaning and the flow of what had happened. The sequence of ideas across those days mattered, and by rearranging them, the AI had subtly rewritten the story.

I almost missed it. The output was confident, well-structured, and plausible. It wasn't obviously wrong—it was *quietly* wrong, in a way that would have slipped past anyone who wasn't there. AI generates confident-sounding text whether it's accurate or not. The same authoritative tone accompanies correct facts and quiet fabrications. You must verify anything that matters, especially factual claims and sequences of events.

"AI is objective because it's not human." AI systems reflect the patterns in their training data, which was created by humans. They can perpetuate biases, miss nuances, and reflect the blind spots of the internet writ large. AI is not a neutral arbiter.

"More advanced AI will fix these problems." Some limitations—like the inability to provide genuine meaning or to verify its own truth-claims—may not be fixable by making AI more sophisticated. These may be fundamental constraints on pattern-recognition systems, regardless of scale.

"AI will replace my job tomorrow." This fear is both overblown and misdirected. A better question: How will AI change what my job involves, and what can I do to stay ahead of that change? We'll explore this in depth in Part 4, but the short answer is that adaptation—not avoidance—is the path forward.

A Grounded Way Forward

So how should you think about AI going forward?

Treat AI as a capable assistant, not an authority. AI can help you draft, analyze, research, and organize. It cannot replace your judgment on matters that require values, context, or genuine understanding. When I use AI for board presentations, it organizes the information—but I decide what it means and what we should do about it.

Verify what matters. For casual tasks, AI outputs are often fine as-is. For anything where accuracy matters—facts you'll cite, decisions with real consequences, professional advice—verify through reliable sources.

Invest in the skills AI can't replicate. Critical thinking. Value-based judgment. Creative vision. The ability to ask good questions. The skill of learning itself. These become more, not less, valuable as AI handles routine cognitive tasks.

Stay curious without being credulous. AI capabilities are genuinely expanding. New applications emerge regularly. But not every announcement represents a fundamental breakthrough. The ability to distinguish signal from noise in AI coverage is itself a valuable skill.

The people who understand what AI actually is—and what it isn't—will be the ones who use it best. And using it well starts with the grounded understanding this chapter provides.

Chapter Summary

Key takeaways:

- AI is pattern recognition at scale—not consciousness, not genuine understanding
- AI excels at processing information, generating drafts, finding patterns, and automating routine work
- AI cannot provide meaning, verify its own outputs, reason about truly novel situations, or maintain understanding across contexts
- The gap between AI hype and reality is significant; transformation is happening, but not at the pace headlines suggest
- Critical thinking, value-based judgment, and the ability to ask good questions become more valuable as AI handles routine cognitive tasks

A question to sit with:

If AI could do 80% of your current work tomorrow, what would you grieve? What would you celebrate? Your answer reveals what you really value about your work.

What's next: In Chapter 2, we'll explore the spectrum of AI autonomy—from simple autocomplete to sophisticated agents—and help you understand where different AI tools fit and when to use each level.

"If you can critically think, upskill properly, and take ownership, you'll always have a job."

Chapter 2: The Autonomy Spectrum

I was on a video call showing a friend how I build software, and I realized I was demonstrating three completely different relationships with AI in the span of five minutes.

First, I opened my coding tool and told it to build a comprehensive test suite for my app. Sixteen tasks appeared on screen, and the AI started executing them one by one—reading files, writing code, running tests, fixing problems—all without any input from me. I went back to the conversation while it worked in the background.

Then my friend asked about a technical concept from a board governance class we'd taken together—something about the business judgment rule and two related legal standards. He couldn't remember the other two. I opened my AI assistant and asked: "I had a class last week where the business judgment rule was discussed along with two other standards. What were they?" It searched through my recorded conversations, found the lecture, and gave him the answer in seconds.

Meanwhile, my phone's keyboard was auto-completing words as I typed a quick text to my wife about dinner.

Three AI interactions. Three completely different levels of autonomy. The phone keyboard was guessing my next word. The assistant was answering a specific question. And the coding agent was independently planning and executing a complex multi-step project. Understanding this spectrum isn't academic—it determines which tool to reach for, how much attention it deserves, and whether you can trust the output.

CHAPTER OVERVIEW

What you'll learn: - The five levels of AI autonomy - Where common AI tools fit on the spectrum - How to match autonomy level to different tasks - When to give AI more or less independence

Why it matters: The right level of AI autonomy makes you more productive; the wrong level creates problems.

Reading time: About 12 minutes

From Autocomplete to Autonomous

Think of AI assistance as a spectrum with five levels, from least to most autonomous:

Level 1: Autocomplete – The AI predicts your next keystroke or word. You're in complete control; the AI just makes typing faster. This is what happens when your phone suggests "the" after you type "in" or when your email finishes a common phrase.

Level 2: Suggestion – The AI offers ideas you can accept, reject, or modify. You might ask "What are some ways to start this email?" and get three options. You choose which (if any) to use.

Level 3: Conversation – The AI engages in back-and-forth dialogue, answering questions, explaining concepts, and helping you think through problems. This is what most people experience with ChatGPT or Claude—a conversation where you ask and the AI responds.

Level 4: Agent – The AI can plan multi-step tasks, take actions across different systems, and report back. You describe what you want;

the AI figures out how to do it. It might read documents, search for information, write files, and pull together results—all without needing your input at each step.

Level 5: Autonomous – The AI works toward goals with minimal supervision, making decisions and taking actions independently. This level is still emerging and requires significant trust and governance structures.

Most of your daily AI interactions probably fall at Levels 2 and 3. But Level 4—what some call "agentic" AI—is becoming increasingly practical and powerful. I live in Level 4 most of the time now, and it's transformed what I can accomplish.

> **KEY POINT**
>
> Higher autonomy isn't automatically better. The right level depends on the task, the stakes, and how much you trust the AI's judgment in that specific domain.

Understanding Each Level

Here's how each level works in practice.

Level 1: Autocomplete

How it works: The AI predicts what comes next based on what you've typed and common patterns. It sees only a few words or characters of context.

Examples: - Phone keyboard suggestions - Basic code completion in programming tools - Search engine query completion

Your role: You accept or ignore suggestions keystroke by keystroke. You maintain complete control.

Best for: Routine typing where speed matters and the stakes are low.

Level 2: Suggestion

How it works: The AI generates options based on a brief description of what you need. You review and choose.

Examples: - "Suggest three subject lines for this email" - "Give me five ways to phrase this sentence" - Image editing tools that suggest enhancements

Your role: You evaluate options and decide which (if any) to use. You provide minimal context; the AI fills in gaps with general patterns.

Best for: Creative tasks where you want options to react to, not blank-page creation.

Level 3: Conversation

How it works: You engage in dialogue with the AI. You can ask follow-up questions, request clarification, push back on answers, and refine results through iteration.

Examples: - ChatGPT, Claude, or similar assistants - Customer service chatbots - Research assistants that answer questions

Your role: You guide the conversation, evaluate responses, and decide when you have what you need. You can provide significant context through the dialogue.

Best for: Research, explanation, brainstorming, drafting, and any task where back-and-forth refinement improves results.

This is where I started with AI, and it's still where I go for thinking through problems. When I was preparing a comprehensive corporate analysis for a board of directors, I spent hours in conversation mode—asking questions, pushing back on AI's initial analysis, providing additional context, and gradually building a nuanced understanding. The AI wasn't doing the work autonomously; we were thinking together.

TRY THIS

Take a task you'd normally do with a single prompt ("Write me an email about...") and try it as a conversation instead. Start with "I need to write an email. Before I give you the details, what information would help you write a better draft?" Notice how the resulting email differs from the single-prompt approach.

Level 4: Agent

How it works: You describe a goal, and the AI figures out how to get there. It breaks the work into steps, executes them across multiple tools and systems, and reports back with results or asks for your input at decision points.

This is where my relationship with AI fundamentally changed. I don't know how to code—at least not in the traditional sense. But I told my AI coding agent what I wanted to build: a personal AI assistant that listens to conversations, integrates health data, maintains a digital memory of my life, and uses cutting-edge encryption. I described the architecture I wanted, the user experience, the features. The agent planned how to implement each piece, wrote the code, set up the servers, configured the databases, and built it. I came back and reviewed the results. When something wasn't right, I described what needed to change and it went back to work.

I built an entire application ecosystem this way—the app, a website, cloud infrastructure, security monitoring systems—everything built by an AI agent executing my vision while I focused on the design decisions that actually required my judgment.

Examples: - Research assistants that gather and synthesize information autonomously - AI coding tools that modify multiple files to implement a feature - Business intelligence tools that analyze data and generate insights

Your role: You define the goal clearly, provide necessary context, and review results. You intervene when the AI makes wrong assumptions or needs decisions.

Best for: Complex tasks that would require many individual requests if done conversationally. Tasks where you trust the AI's judgment within defined boundaries.

Level 5: Autonomous

How it works: The AI works toward broad goals with significant independence. It might manage ongoing processes, make judgment calls, and adapt to changing circumstances without explicit instruction.

I got a taste of this when I built an AI-powered security monitoring system. I gave it access to scanning tools, threat databases, and defensive capabilities, then told it: monitor my infrastructure, detect threats, and respond. One day I checked in and found it had detected a brute force attack, blocked the threat, and logged the incident—all without me knowing it was happening. It was running attacks against my own systems to find vulnerabilities—using the same tools that real hackers would use, but doing it autonomously to make my defenses stronger.

Examples: - Security monitoring systems that detect and respond to threats - Autonomous trading systems - Self-driving vehicle decision-making - Emerging "AI agents" that manage complex workflows

Your role: You set goals and boundaries, monitor outcomes, and intervene when things go wrong. You don't guide individual actions.

Best for: Situations where AI judgment is well-established and trustworthy, where human oversight at each step is impractical, and where appropriate governance exists.

Important caution: Most individual users should be very selective about Level 5 autonomy. The stakes and the trust required are high. Even my security AI occasionally crashes or needs reconfiguration—and I built it understanding the risks. Start lower on the spectrum and work your way up as you develop trust and understanding.

Matching Autonomy to Task

Here's a practical framework for deciding how much autonomy to give AI for different tasks:

Lower autonomy (Levels 1-2) when: - The stakes are high and errors are costly - You have strong preferences that are hard to articulate - You want to stay actively engaged with the work - The task requires nuanced judgment you don't trust AI to have - You're learning and want to understand the process

Higher autonomy (Levels 3-4) when: - The task is well-defined with clear success criteria - Errors can be caught and corrected before causing harm - You trust AI judgment in this specific domain - The task involves processing large amounts of information - Your time is better spent reviewing than doing

In my experience, this maps well to how you'd work with a competent new employee. Would you give them this task with this level of independence? If you'd want to check their work at each step, use lower autonomy. If you'd say "figure it out and report back," higher autonomy makes sense.

I shift between levels constantly, even within the same project. When I'm building software, the AI operates as an agent—planning tasks, writing code, executing builds. That's Level 4. But when I'm deciding *what* to build, I drop to Level 3 and think through the implications in conversation. And when I'm reviewing what the AI produced, I'm paying close attention to every detail—essentially back at Level 2, evaluating suggestions one by one. The stakes determine the autonomy: execution can be autonomous, but design decisions require my judgment.

THINK ABOUT IT

Consider the AI tools you currently use. Where do they fall on this spectrum? Are you using them at the right level of autonomy, or might you benefit from adjusting your approach—giving more independence where appropriate, or staying more involved where stakes are higher?

The Collaboration Continuum

Here's the insight that changed how I think about AI tools: the autonomy spectrum isn't really about AI—it's about collaboration. The question isn't "How much should AI do?" but "How should we work together on this?"

High human involvement, low AI autonomy: - You do most of the thinking; AI accelerates execution - Example: You write an email; AI suggests better phrasing for specific sentences - Best when your judgment and voice matter most

Balanced collaboration: - You and AI iterate together toward a result - Example: You describe what you want; AI drafts; you refine; AI adjusts; repeat - Best for most knowledge work tasks

Low human involvement, high AI autonomy: - AI does most of the work; you review and approve - Example: AI researches a topic, synthesizes findings, and presents conclusions - Best when AI can reliably handle the task and your time is the constraint

Most effective AI use involves conscious movement along this continuum. You might start with high collaboration (defining the problem together) and then shift to higher autonomy (AI executes while you do other things) and then back to high collaboration (refining results together). That's exactly what happened when I showed my friend the coding agent building sixteen tasks while we kept talking—the agent handled the execution while I focused on the conversation that needed my human presence.

Common Mistakes

Over-automation: Giving AI too much autonomy for tasks that require human judgment. This often happens because automation feels efficient—but efficiency doesn't matter if the output isn't right.

Example: Letting AI draft and send customer responses without review. Fast, but you lose quality control and personal touch.

Under-automation: Keeping AI at low autonomy for tasks it could handle more independently. This often comes from lack of trust or unfamiliarity with what AI can do.

Example: Manually guiding each step of research AI could do autonomously, spending an hour on what could take ten minutes.

Fixed autonomy: Using the same level of autonomy for everything. Different tasks warrant different approaches, even within the same project.

Example: Always using conversation mode when sometimes suggestion mode (faster) or agent mode (more comprehensive) would be better.

Invisible autonomy creep: Gradually letting AI take more control without conscious decision. Today you review everything; six months later, you're barely glancing at AI outputs before using them.

Example: Initially reviewing every AI-drafted email carefully, then skimming, then trusting completely—without ever deciding to make that shift. We saw this in our developer pilot—teams who started with careful code review gradually relaxed their oversight. The ones who recognized the drift and made conscious decisions about it did fine. The ones who didn't notice sometimes ended up with AI-generated code that pulled in external packages or introduced security vulnerabilities they hadn't vetted.

Practical Guidelines

Start lower, scale up: When working with a new AI tool or task type, begin with more human involvement. As you learn what the AI does well, consciously increase autonomy.

Match autonomy to stakes: Higher-stakes decisions warrant lower autonomy. A creative brainstorm can be highly autonomous; a legal document should not be.

Build in checkpoints: Even with higher autonomy, include moments where you review direction before the AI continues. This catches problems early. When my coding agent is building something complex, I have it pause and show me the plan before executing—not because I don't trust it, but because a wrong assumption caught early saves hours of rework.

Trust, but verify: You can trust AI to do good work without trusting it to be always correct. Review matters for errors, even when you generally trust the output.

Know your defaults: Most people develop default autonomy levels for different tasks. Make these conscious choices rather than habits you never examine.

Why This Matters

The people who thrive with AI won't be those who use the most autonomous tools. They'll be those who consciously choose the right level of autonomy for each situation—engaging closely where human judgment matters, stepping back where AI can handle the work, and knowing the difference.

When I told my friend "I don't know how to code," his response was: "That doesn't matter. You know what needs to be built. You know all the pieces. You just tell it what to do." He was describing the shift from doing to directing—from 'I need to write every line myself' to 'I need to define what success looks like and let the AI execute.'

As AI tools become more capable, that shift becomes available to everyone. It isn't something to fear—it's an opportunity to focus your energy where it matters most.

Chapter Summary

Key takeaways:

- AI autonomy exists on a spectrum from simple autocomplete to fully autonomous agents
- Each level has appropriate use cases; higher isn't automatically better
- Match autonomy level to task stakes, your trust in AI judgment, and the nature of the work
- Most effective AI use involves conscious movement along the spectrum based on the task at hand
- Watch for invisible autonomy creep—make deliberate choices about how much independence to give AI
- As AI becomes more capable, your skill shifts from doing to directing

What's next: In Chapter 3, we'll explore mental models for thinking about AI—frameworks that help you develop intuition for when to use AI, how much to trust it, and how to get the best results from human-AI collaboration.

"The question isn't 'can AI do this?' but 'how should we work together on this?'"

Chapter 3: How to Think About AI

I was at a Gartner conference when an analyst said something that changed the way I think about AI entirely. He was talking about the future of software development, and he used the metaphor of an orchestra conductor.

In the past, he said, a developer had to play every instrument—tuba, violin, drums—or you needed a team where each person specialized in one. But with agentic development tools, the role shifts. The developer becomes more like a conductor. The conductor understands the score, understands the music, understands the outcomes, understands how all the pieces flow together and how they should sound. His job is to turn notes on a page and fifty-plus musicians into something incredible.

I latched onto that metaphor immediately. It felt right. But I'll tell you something: knowing the right mental model and living it are two very different things. It took me months of learning, failing, and iterating to truly understand what that conductor role means in practice—and I'm still learning. What I did nine months ago looks crude compared to how I work now. Just like a real conductor needs to know music theory, understand instruments, and spend years refining their craft, being effective with AI still takes real time, growth, and learning.

This chapter is about those mental models—the frameworks that help you think clearly about when to use AI, what to expect, and how to get the most from human-AI collaboration.

CHAPTER OVERVIEW

What you'll learn: - Mental models that improve AI interactions - The "brilliant but inexperienced colleague" framework - When AI excels versus when humans excel - How to develop AI intuition through practice

Why it matters: The right mental model is often more valuable than the right prompt.

Reading time: About 15 minutes

The Mental Model Problem

Most people approach AI with a mental model they've never examined. These models come from our experience with other technologies:

The search engine model: You type a query; the AI finds and returns information. This model leads people to ask single questions and accept the first response as the answer.

The calculator model: You input data; the AI processes it deterministically. This model leads people to expect AI to be perfectly reliable and to distrust it when it's not.

The magic 8-ball model: You ask a question; you get an answer; whether it's useful is somewhat random. This model leads people to accept whatever AI says without verification.

The junior employee model: You give detailed instructions; the AI executes exactly as told. This model leads people to over-specify requests and miss AI's ability to contribute judgment.

None of these models is entirely wrong, but none captures what makes AI genuinely powerful. I know because I worked through most of them myself. My earliest attempts at using AI for serious work were basically the search engine model—ask a question, get an answer, move on. When I started building software, I shifted to the junior employee model—give extremely detailed instructions and hope for exact execution. For my first attempts, I didn't do enough creative thinking, critical thinking, and planning up front, and I ended up with a mediocre, buggy app.

The conductor model changed everything. But it took time for that metaphor to become practice.

The Brilliant But Inexperienced Colleague

In practical terms, here's the mental model that actually works: **think of AI as a brilliant but inexperienced colleague.**

This colleague has read extensively about almost every topic. They can write clearly, analyze data, spot patterns, and work incredibly fast. They're eager to help and never get tired.

But they have significant limitations. They've never worked at your company. They don't know your specific goals, constraints, or preferences unless you tell them. They sometimes confuse general knowledge with specific facts. They're confident even when they shouldn't be. And they lack the judgment that comes from lived experience.

Someone once asked me how I built an entire AI-powered personal assistant app when I don't know how to code. "I just used something called Cursor," I said. "I tell it what I want to do." Their response captured something important: "Those are the smartest people—the ones who know what they need and can give it to somebody or something that can translate that into something meaningful."

That's the colleague model in action. I know the architecture, the user experience, the security requirements, the business logic. AI knows the programming languages, the APIs, the implementation details. When I work with AI like a colleague—providing the context, judgment, and direction while leveraging its processing power and breadth of knowledge—the results are dramatically better than either of us could produce alone.

When you work with this colleague:

You provide context they can't know. A real colleague who's new to your company needs orientation. They need to understand your goals, your constraints, your preferences, and why things are done the way they're done. AI needs the same orientation, except you have to provide it explicitly every time (or build systems to provide it automatically, which we'll cover in later chapters).

You leverage their strengths. Your brilliant colleague can process information faster than you can, spot patterns you'd miss, and generate options you wouldn't have considered. Use them for what they're good at. When we ran a pilot program with fifty developers using AI coding tools, they reported 5x faster delivery on new projects, with 80-90% of AI suggestions rated as useful. That's the kind of leverage this colleague provides.

You compensate for their weaknesses. You verify their work when accuracy matters. You provide judgment they lack. You catch the cases where their inexperience leads them astray. The same pilot found that requirements and context matter most—the developers who invested in clear specifications up front got dramatically better results than those who just started typing.

You collaborate, not delegate. The best results come from working together—your judgment and context combined with their processing power and broad knowledge.

TRY THIS

Think of a recent AI interaction that went poorly. Now reimagine it through the "brilliant but inexperienced colleague" lens. What context did you fail to provide? What judgment did you assume the AI would have? How might you approach the same task differently?

Two Ways of Knowing

C.S. Lewis described two ways of knowing: looking AT something—analyzing it from the outside—and looking ALONG something—experiencing it from the inside. AI is excellent at the first and cannot do the second.

I experienced this distinction viscerally during my first major AI research project.

I was doing a comprehensive analysis of CoreCivic, a company that operates private prisons and detention facilities for the federal government—immigration, federal marshals, and more. AI rapidly gave me the ability to look AT CoreCivic: their financials, their corporate structure, what was being said on Glassdoor, what the media was saying, what society was saying on social media. It was thorough, structured, and impressively fast.

But what AI couldn't give me—what came entirely from my own experiences—was a vision of what CoreCivic *could* look like. Is it possible to address the social, ethical, moral, and economic concerns in a fundamentally new way? Are they really delivering value back to society?

What I brought to those questions was every perspective I'd cultivated across my entire life.

There was my business and technology perspective from thirteen years at Booz Allen Hamilton as a management and technology consultant. There was my master's degree at Johns Hopkins Carey School of Business, where case studies and cross-functional analysis expanded my worldview. And then there was Fuller Theological Seminary, where I took a class in global leadership—the only businessman in a room full of NGO leaders, nonprofit directors, and church pastors from across the spectrum of denominations.

One of my classmates was a pastor from Africa. He told his story of growing up on a banana farm where his family was paid in bananas. His view of business people was that they could not be Christians—he simply hadn't seen business creating genuine value in his context. At the end of the class, he told me I'd changed his perspective. And I told him he'd changed mine—about the comprehensive value that businesses should generate for everyone they touch.

When I looked at CoreCivic's data, all of this was in my head. It had become part of who I am. It was natural for me to ask: How can CoreCivic drive value to shareholders *while* driving value to society, its employees, and its customers? My first conclusion was that CoreCivic needed to redefine who its customers are. If it approaches its customers as the people who are incarcerated—not just the government agencies paying the bills—it drives a completely different narrative about outcomes.

I remembered Dave's Killer Bread—an ex-con who started a bakery at a farmers market, hired exclusively from people coming out of prison, and built a business that Flowers Foods eventually acquired for $250 million. I remembered a group of men in a high-security prison who had been consistently beating Ivy League debate teams, including Harvard. All that untapped human potential.

None of this came from AI. AI couldn't connect a seminary classroom in Pasadena to a bread company in Portland to a debate team behind bars to a corporate strategy for a prison operator. That kind of thinking—weaving lived experience, ethical conviction, and cross-domain pattern recognition into a genuinely new strategic vision—is what Lewis meant by looking ALONG.

AI excels at looking AT: - Analyzing patterns in data - Summarizing information from multiple sources - Identifying logical structures in arguments - Comparing options against stated criteria - Explaining how things work

Humans excel at looking ALONG: - Knowing what it feels like to face a difficult choice - Understanding why something matters to you

- Recognizing what's appropriate in a specific social context - Sensing when something is "off" even if you can't explain why - Connecting knowledge to personal experience and meaning

The most effective AI use combines both: AI analyzes while you experience. AI processes while you judge. AI generates options while you decide what matters.

In many cases, AI is like the employee who's great at pointing out problems everyone already knows but offers no solutions and no willingness to work toward one. AI can't make the leap of looking *along* the data to envision something better. That leap requires you.

KEY POINT

AI can tell you *that* something is true. It struggles to tell you *why it matters* or *what you should do about it*. Those questions require the kind of knowing that comes from lived experience.

When AI Excels

We covered AI's specific capabilities in Chapter 1. Here, the question is different: not *what* AI can do, but *what type of thinking* it handles well—so you can recognize those moments in your own work.

The pattern is consistent: AI excels at tasks that involve processing, comparing, and generating at scale. Information synthesis, pattern recognition across large data sets, first-draft generation, and rapid iteration are all tasks where AI's speed and breadth make a real difference.

A couple of years ago, my security operations center director came to me with an unexpected problem. "We no longer have a junior SOC," he said. Machine learning and automation had taken over all the deterministic, if-this-then-that work that junior analysts used to do. We were automating hundreds of thousands of events end-to-end, leaving only a few thousand actual incidents that required human attention.

His concern was real: we had junior people whose entire job category was being automated away. My answer was that we needed to accelerate their growth—get them to mid-level and senior capabilities as fast as possible—because all the low-value, repetitive work was gone. The high-value work—judgment calls, complex investigations, strategic thinking—remained.

That's the pattern everywhere. When I catch myself spending an hour on something that involves assembling information from multiple sources, that's my signal to hand it to AI.

When Humans Excel

Understanding where AI falls short helps you protect the value you bring:

Value-based judgment. Deciding what matters, what's worth pursuing, and how to weigh competing goods. AI can tell you the implications of different choices; it cannot tell you which choice is right for you.

Relational intelligence. Understanding people, building trust, navigating relationships. AI can suggest what to say; only you can sense when to say it, how to say it, and what the other person really needs to hear.

Creative vision. Imagining something that doesn't exist. AI can generate variations on existing patterns; genuine creative breakthroughs come from human imagination seeing possibilities AI wouldn't conceive. Recently I was listening to my friend Hannah Park, a professor who works with dance, talk about how she thinks about AI as a tool in the creative process. It gave me an entirely new perspective—a variation on the conductor theme. My conclusion is that ultimately a lot of our technical tasks are going to become much more creative endeavors as we learn to conduct and dance through our work while using AI.

Ethical judgment in context. Knowing what's right in this specific situation, with these specific people, given this specific history. AI can apply general ethical principles; you have to decide what matters when principles conflict.

Meaning-making. Connecting work to purpose, finding significance in difficulty, understanding why something matters. AI operates in a universe of optimization; humans live in a universe of meaning. My CoreCivic analysis wasn't just about financial returns—it was about whether a company could transform an industry while honoring the dignity of every person it touches. That question requires a kind of thinking AI simply doesn't have.

Tacit knowledge. The skills you can't articulate—knowing when a deal feels wrong, sensing when a project is going off track, recognizing quality in your field. This accumulated judgment is hard to transfer to AI because you can't fully explain it yourself.

As AI advances, I don't think it's going to replace human beings as much as people fear. I think it is going to force us back to the fundamentals of what it means to truly think, create, and communicate. The premium isn't on knowing facts—AI has that covered. The premium is on having something worth saying and knowing how to say it.

> **THINK ABOUT IT**
>
> Consider your work. What parts require value-based judgment, relational intelligence, or meaning-making? These are where your human contribution matters most. What parts involve information processing, pattern recognition, or iteration? These are candidates for AI assistance.

Developing AI Intuition

Here's what I've learned from working with AI daily for over a year: you develop intuition. A sense of when AI will help, when it won't, and how to get good results. This intuition comes from practice, but you can accelerate it.

The conductor metaphor sounds easy, but the gap between understanding it intellectually and living it is enormous. What I did nine months ago—asking basic questions, accepting first responses, giving minimal context—I now recognize as barely scratching the surface. Today I work differently: detailed specifications up front, iterative refinement, memory systems that maintain context across sessions, verification for accuracy. The results are better, faster, and more meaningful.

Notice what works. When an AI interaction goes well, ask yourself why. Was it the way you framed the request? The context you provided? The type of task? Build a mental catalog of what works.

Notice what fails. When AI disappoints, don't just move on. Understand why. Was it a context problem (AI didn't know something it needed to)? A capability problem (AI can't do this type of task well)? A judgment problem (AI applied the wrong approach)?

Experiment with approaches. Try the same task multiple ways. Single prompt versus conversation. Detailed instructions versus high-level goals. More context versus less. The variance in results teaches you what matters.

Learn the tool's quirks. Every AI system has tendencies—patterns in how it interprets requests, common ways it goes wrong, tricks that reliably help. These quirks aren't documented; you learn them through use.

Calibrate your trust. Over time, you learn which AI outputs you can trust without verification and which require checking. This calibrated trust lets you move faster without taking on excessive risk.

Practical Mental Models

Beyond the "brilliant colleague" frame, here are other useful ways to think about AI:

AI as thought partner. When you're working through a complex problem, treat AI as someone to think with. Explain your reasoning out loud (in text). Ask it to challenge your assumptions. Use it to explore possibilities you haven't considered.

AI as first reader. Before sharing work with others, have AI review it. "What's unclear in this proposal? What questions would a skeptical reader have? What am I missing?" AI provides a safe testing ground.

AI as research librarian. When you need to understand a topic, treat AI like a knowledgeable librarian who can point you to the right resources, explain complex concepts, and help you form good questions.

AI as efficiency multiplier. For routine tasks, think of AI as a way to get 80% of the result with 20% of the effort. The final 20% might still need your attention, but you've saved significant time.

AI as safety net. For work that might have errors, use AI as a check. "Review this document for logical inconsistencies." "What mistakes might I have made in this analysis?" AI catches what you might miss.

The Question That Matters

In a world where AI can access virtually any information, the premium shifts to knowing what questions to ask.

Questions AI can help answer: - What does this data show? - How does this system work? - What are the options for solving this problem? - What have others done in similar situations? - What am I missing in my analysis?

Questions only you can answer: - What do I actually want? -

What matters most in this situation? - What risks am I willing to take? - How does this connect to what I value? - What would success really mean to me?

The first set of questions drives effective AI use. The second set drives effective life. AI handles the information; you provide the direction.

Chapter Summary

Key takeaways:

- The mental model you bring to AI interactions shapes what you get out of them
- Think of AI as a "brilliant but inexperienced colleague" or yourself as a conductor—capable, but requiring your context, judgment, and direction
- AI excels at "looking AT" (analysis, pattern recognition, processing); humans excel at "looking ALONG" (meaning, judgment, lived experience)
- The gap between understanding a mental model and living it takes months of deliberate practice
- As AI handles more routine cognitive work, the premium shifts to creativity, meaning-making, and the fundamentals of human thinking
- Developing AI intuition requires deliberate attention to what works and what doesn't

What's next: Part 2 explores the practical techniques for working with AI—how to provide context effectively, communicate clearly, and build productive human-AI collaboration patterns.

"The question isn't 'can you code?' but 'do you know what you want, and can you ask good questions?'"

Chapter 4: Working With AI, Not Against It

For months, my AI results were mediocre.

I'd ask Claude to help with board presentations, strategy documents, research summaries. What I got back was... fine. Generic. The kind of output that required so much revision I sometimes wondered if I should have just written it myself.

I treated AI like a search engine with better grammar. Type a question, get an answer, move on. The results reflected that approach: surface-level, one-size-fits-none responses that missed the specific context of my work.

Then I changed how I worked.

Instead of asking "Write me an executive summary of our security posture," I started with: "I need to create an executive summary for our board. Before we start, let me tell you about our situation..." I described our organization, the board's concerns, what we'd accomplished, where we still had gaps, and what I needed them to understand.

The AI's next response wasn't perfect, but it was *relevant*. It asked clarifying questions. It proposed a structure I could actually work with. Over thirty minutes of back-and-forth, we developed a document that would have taken me a full day to create alone—and it fit my specific situation. That first draft wasn't the final product, but it gave me a foundation worth iterating on. After several more rounds of refinement—grounding the presentation in our organization's actual context—I had something genuinely impactful.

I hadn't found a better AI tool. I'd found a better way to work *with* the tool I had.

> **CHAPTER OVERVIEW**
>
> **What you'll learn:** - The difference between using AI as a tool versus working with it as a partner - The plan-execute-verify loop that drives better results - How to set AI up for success with your requests - Why verification remains your responsibility
>
> **Why it matters:** The same AI tool can give wildly different results depending on how you work with it.
>
> **Reading time:** About 15 minutes

The Old Way and the New Way

Most people use AI the way they'd use a search engine: type a question, get an answer, done. This approach treats AI as a vending machine—insert query, receive output.

The vending machine approach works for simple tasks. "What's the capital of France?" needs no conversation. "Summarize this article" requires minimal context. For these tasks, ask and answer is fine.

But for meaningful work, this approach leaves most of AI's value on the table.

The old way: - Ask a single question - Accept whatever comes back - Do significant work yourself to adapt the output - Start over if the result isn't useful

The new way: - Treat AI as a working partner - Provide context about your situation - Engage in back-and-forth refinement - Build toward results collaboratively

The shift isn't about learning fancy prompting techniques. It's about changing your relationship with the tool—from transaction to collaboration. Remember the "brilliant but inexperienced colleague" from Chapter 3? You wouldn't hand a new team member a one-line request and expect a perfect result. You'd brief them, discuss the approach, and refine together.

> **KEY POINT**
>
> You get out of AI what you put into the relationship. A single query gets a generic response. A thoughtful collaboration gets a tailored result.

The Plan-Execute-Verify Loop

Effective AI work follows a rhythm I call the **plan-execute-verify loop**. Whether you're using AI for research, writing, analysis, or problem-solving, this pattern produces better results.

Step 1: Plan

Before diving into execution, establish a shared understanding of what you're trying to accomplish.

This might look like: - Explaining your goal and constraints - Asking AI to propose an approach - Discussing what good looks like - Agreeing on how you'll work together

For my board summary, this was the opening conversation—describing the organization, the audience, the challenges, and what success would look like. The AI couldn't have produced a relevant document without this foundation.

Why planning matters: AI doesn't know what you know. Without planning, it fills gaps with assumptions—often wrong ones. Planning surfaces these gaps before they cause problems.

Step 2: Execute

With a plan in place, move into producing actual work. This might be: - AI drafting content while you guide - Working through sections systematically - Generating options for your review - Iterating on deliverables

The execution phase often involves multiple cycles. AI produces something; you respond with feedback; AI refines; you refine further. This iteration is normal and valuable.

I was preparing a board presentation on our security posture—the kind of high-stakes deliverable where generic slides would be worse than useless. After the planning phase, where I'd briefed the AI on our organization, the board's concerns, and what I needed them to understand, we moved into execution.

The first draft had the right structure but was too long—fifteen pages that no board member would sit through. I told the AI: "This covers everything, but it's too long. The board cares about three things: risk reduction progress, remaining gaps, and what we need from them. Cut everything else." The next version was tighter but still had a weak opening. "Start with the metric they'll care about most—how many fewer incidents are reaching our analysts." Better.

Then my boss reviewed it and had his own strong opinions about what the board needed to hear. I brought that feedback straight back to the AI: "My boss wants more emphasis on the cost avoidance numbers and less on the technical architecture details. Here's his specific input..." Another round of iteration. Fifteen pages became six—each one sharp, focused, and grounded in the numbers that would matter in that room.

The presentation was extremely well received. Not because AI wrote something brilliant on the first try, but because we iterated—back and forth, feedback and refinement—until the result fit that specific audience and moment.

Why iteration matters: First outputs are rarely final outputs. The back-and-forth isn't inefficiency—it's how you and AI converge on what you actually need.

Step 3: Verify

Before using any AI output for real purposes, verify it meets your standards.

Verification includes: - Checking facts that matter - Ensuring the output fits your context - Reviewing for tone and appropriateness - Confirming alignment with your goals

For that board presentation, verification meant checking every metric against our actual dashboards, confirming the language matched how our board chair typically framed security issues, and reading each slide aloud to test whether it sounded like something I'd actually say in the boardroom. Two numbers needed correction. One recommendation was subtly off-target. Without verification, I'd have presented polished-looking content that could have undermined my credibility.

Why verification matters: AI can produce confident-sounding outputs that are wrong. Your verification catches what AI can't. This isn't distrust—it's appropriate professional responsibility.

Then the loop continues: verified outputs inform the next planning phase, or reveal issues that require adjustment. You'll see this pattern surface throughout the rest of the book—in research (Chapter 8), decision-making (Chapter 9), and workplace applications (Chapter 10).

> **TRY THIS**
>
> Take a task you'd normally approach with a single AI prompt. Instead, explicitly follow the plan-execute-verify loop: 1. **Plan:** Spend 2-3 messages establishing context and agreeing on an approach 2. **Execute:** Work through

the task collaboratively, iterating as needed 3. **Verify:** Review the output critically before using it

Compare this result to what a single prompt would have produced.

Setting AI Up for Success

Here's a truth that took me a while to learn: when AI gives you a bad result, it's often because you set it up to fail.

AI doesn't know: - What company you work for - Your role and responsibilities - Your preferences and standards - What you've already tried - Why you're asking this particular question - What constraints you're working within - What "good" looks like for this task

When you provide none of this context, AI has to guess—and its guesses are based on general patterns, not your specific situation.

Setting AI up for success means:

Explain who you are. "I'm a marketing manager at a mid-sized healthcare company" gives AI far better grounding than starting cold.

Explain what you're trying to accomplish. "I need to create a quarterly report for our board" is more useful than "Write a report."

Explain your constraints. "We have a limited budget and need something implementable within 60 days" shapes what AI suggests.

Explain what you've already done. "I've drafted an outline, but I'm struggling with the analysis section" focuses AI's help.

Explain what success looks like. "A good result would be clear, concise, and backed by specific data points" gives AI evaluation criteria.

This context takes thirty seconds to provide. The difference in results can be dramatic.

The Power of Questions

One of the most underused AI techniques is simply asking AI what it needs to know.

Instead of guessing what context to provide, try: "I need help with [task]. Before we start, what information would help you give me the best result?"

AI will ask relevant questions. Your answers build the context you might not have thought to provide. This simple technique—asking what's needed before jumping in—consistently improves outcomes.

Similarly, when AI produces something that misses the mark, instead of starting over, ask: "What assumptions did you make that might explain why this doesn't fit my situation?" The answer often reveals context gaps you can then fill.

> **KEY POINT**
>
> Asking AI what it needs to know is often more valuable than guessing what to tell it.

Common Patterns That Fail

Here are patterns I see repeatedly that produce poor results:

The drive-by request. "Write me a presentation about our product." No context, no constraints, no direction. AI produces something generic that requires so much revision it would have been faster to start from scratch.

The over-specified request. "Write exactly 347 words about innovation, using the following specific phrases, in this exact order, with these formatting requirements." Over-specification removes AI's ability to apply judgment and often produces awkward, stilted outputs.

The no-feedback loop. User gets an imperfect result, throws it away, starts over with a different request. Each restart loses the learning from the previous attempt. Refinement is almost always better than restarting.

The unexamined output. User accepts AI output without review, uses it for real purposes, discovers problems later. Verification isn't optional—it's part of the workflow.

The wrong autonomy level. Asking AI to make decisions that require your judgment, or micromanaging tasks AI could handle more independently. Match the autonomy level to the task (see Chapter 2).

What Remains Your Job

Working with AI doesn't mean abdicating responsibility. Certain things remain firmly in your domain:

Judgment calls. AI can present options and analyze tradeoffs. Deciding what matters most, which risks are acceptable, and what direction to take—that's you.

Quality standards. AI doesn't know your standards until you express them. Maintaining quality requires your attention, especially for important work.

Verification. Checking facts, confirming appropriateness, ensuring fit with context—these are human responsibilities.

Accountability. If you use AI-generated content, you're responsible for it. "The AI did it" isn't a defense. In my experience—whether in cybersecurity governance or organizational leadership—the person with authority bears the responsibility, regardless of what tools they use.

Final decisions. AI can help you think through decisions. Making them is your job.

Think of it this way: AI can be a brilliant collaborator, but you remain the project lead. You set direction, maintain standards, and own outcomes.

Building a Working Relationship

Over time, effective AI users develop what feels like a working relationship with their tools. This isn't anthropomorphizing—it's recognizing that good collaboration requires adapting to your tools, just as they adapt to your inputs.

You learn the AI's tendencies. What it does well, where it struggles, what kinds of requests produce good results. This learning makes you more effective.

You develop shared patterns. Ways of working that consistently produce results. Phrases that reliably communicate what you need. Approaches that fit your style.

You build on previous work. In longer sessions, early conversation informs later collaboration. What you established in planning carries through execution.

You adjust as needed. When results drift from expectations, you course-correct. When AI seems stuck, you try different approaches.

This isn't magic—it's the same dynamic that makes any working relationship productive. Investment in the relationship pays dividends in results.

> **THINK ABOUT IT**
>
> Consider a professional relationship you have that works well. What makes it effective? How do you communicate, set expectations, and handle misalignments? Now consider how those same elements might apply to working with AI.

Practical Starting Points

If you're new to this approach, start here:

Before your next AI task: 1. Write two sentences about who you are and what you're trying to accomplish 2. Write one sentence about what constraints you're working within 3. Write one sentence about what a good result would look like

That's your opening context. Provide it before making your actual request.

During the task: - Ask AI to propose an approach before diving in - When something misses the mark, refine rather than restart - Provide feedback on what's working and what isn't - Ask questions when you're not sure what's happening

After the task: - Verify anything important before using it - Note what worked and what didn't for future reference - Consider what context you could have provided earlier

These practices transform vending-machine interactions into genuine collaboration.

Chapter Summary

Key takeaways:

- Working with AI as a partner yields dramatically better results than treating it as a query machine
- The plan-execute-verify loop provides structure for effective collaboration
- Setting AI up for success requires providing context it can't know on its own
- Asking AI what information it needs is often more effective than guessing what to provide
- Verification and judgment remain your responsibility, regardless of how good AI becomes

What's next: Chapter 5 explores the art of context in depth—how to provide the right information to AI, how much is enough, and how to build context progressively across longer interactions.

"The question isn't 'can AI do this?' but 'what would AI need from me to do this well?'"

Chapter 5: The Art of Context

I was preparing a security briefing for our board of directors, and the AI-generated draft was technically accurate but completely forgettable. Generic corporate language. The kind of briefing that could have come from any organization in any industry. I knew the material cold—I'd been living with our threat landscape for months—but I was stuck on how to frame it for a non-technical audience with limited attention.

So I tried something different. Instead of asking AI to write the briefing, I told it everything: our specific threat landscape, the board's priorities, what we'd already tried, what had worked and what hadn't, the political dynamics of the room I'd be presenting in. Then I brainstormed out loud with it. Not about content—I had the content. About structure. About how to condense a complex set of concepts into something tight enough to land in twenty minutes.

In the end, I didn't use any of the AI's actual language. But the conversation helped me frame my thoughts in a way that made me ready to craft something impactful. The AI wasn't writing my briefing. It was helping me think through my briefing—but only because it understood enough about my situation to be a useful thinking partner.

That's what context does. It transforms AI from a generic pattern-matcher into something that can genuinely help you think.

CHAPTER OVERVIEW

What you'll learn: - Why context is the single biggest factor in AI results - The five types of context that matter most - How to build context progressively through conversation - How persistent context systems compound value over time

Why it matters: Better context requires no new skills—just awareness of what AI needs to know.

Reading time: About 15 minutes

Why Context Changes Everything

Here's the reality about AI that most users miss: the AI isn't the variable. You are.

When AI gives disappointing results, people often blame the tool. "AI just doesn't understand what I need." "These AI assistants are overrated." "I asked clearly, and it still got it wrong."

But run an experiment: take the same request you made, add context, and try again. The results are often dramatically better—not because the AI improved, but because you gave it what it needed.

I saw this play out at scale. When we ran a pilot program with about fifty developers using AI coding tools across six teams, the single biggest lesson wasn't about which AI model to use or how to write prompts. It was simpler than that: *requirements and context matter most.* The developers who took time to specify what they actually needed—the functionality, the constraints, the standards—got dramatically better results than those who jumped straight to coding. Some built working prototypes in hours that would have taken days. Others fought the same tool and got mediocre output.

Same AI. Same tool. Different context. Different results.

Without context, AI must guess: - Who is asking this question? - What's the real goal behind the request? - What constraints matter? - What level of formality is appropriate? - What's the broader situation?

Every guess is a chance to go wrong. Generic results aren't AI failure—they're AI making safe assumptions when it lacks specific information.

With context, AI can be specific: - This is a CISO presenting to a non-technical board - They need something concise enough for a twenty-minute slot - The board has already seen two generic security presentations this quarter - The goal is to drive a specific investment decision, not just inform - The political dynamics favor framing this as risk management, not technology

The same AI produces entirely different—and much more useful—results.

> **KEY POINT**
>
> When AI gives you generic results, the problem is usually missing context, not AI limitations.

The Five Types of Context

Not all context is created equal. Understanding what types of context matter helps you provide them efficiently.

1. Role Context: Who You Are

AI needs to know who's asking. Your role shapes what kind of help is appropriate.

When I ask AI for help with a security briefing, the output is completely different depending on whether I say "I'm a CISO presenting to our board" versus "I'm a junior analyst preparing a summary for my manager." Same topic. Different calibration—the vocabulary, the level of detail, the assumptions about what I already know.

Examples: - "I'm a senior manager presenting to our board" - "I'm a freelance writer pitching to publications" - "I'm a parent trying to explain this to my teenager" - "I'm new to this field and still learning the basics"

Role context tells AI how to calibrate its response—the vocabulary to use, the level of detail to provide, what assumptions are safe to make.

2. Task Context: What You're Trying to Do

The specific task you're working on, and why it matters.

This is where most people under-invest. "Help me write an email" is task context, but it's thin. "Help me follow up with a client who's been slow to respond—we have a good relationship, but I'm worried this sounds too pushy" gives AI something to actually work with.

In our developer pilot, teams discovered that feeding natural-language descriptions of what they were building—not just code specifications but the purpose, the user experience, the business logic—produced dramatically better results than bare technical requirements. One team fed their planning discussions directly into AI tools and got back structured requirements that needed only human refinement rather than ground-up creation.

Examples: - "I'm writing a proposal to expand our team" - "I need to prepare for a difficult conversation with a colleague" - "I'm trying to understand this technical concept for a presentation" - "I'm organizing a major project and need to create a timeline"

Task context helps AI understand not just what you're asking, but what success looks like.

3. Constraint Context: What Limits Apply

The boundaries within which a solution must work.

Examples: - "Budget is limited to $10,000" - "This needs to be done by Friday" - "The audience has no technical background" - "I can only use tools we already have" - "This must align with our company's values around sustainability"

Constraint context prevents AI from suggesting otherwise-good solutions that don't fit your reality. Without it, you'll get elegant answers that are useless in practice—and waste time explaining why each suggestion won't work.

4. Background Context: Relevant History

What's happened before that informs the current situation.

This is the context type that separates adequate AI interactions from genuinely useful ones. When I started providing background to my AI conversations—our specific threat landscape, what we'd already tried, why previous approaches failed—the output jumped from generic to targeted overnight.

Examples: - "We tried this approach last year and it didn't work because..." - "The client has expressed frustration with response times" - "This team has successfully used similar methods before" - "I've already drafted an outline, which I'll share"

Background context prevents AI from retreading ground you've already covered or missing important lessons from experience. Without it, AI will confidently suggest the exact approach you tried and abandoned six months ago.

5. Success Context: What Good Looks Like

Your criteria for evaluating whether the result is useful.

Examples: - "A good result would be something I can send with minimal editing" - "I need it to be thorough enough to pass legal review" - "This should be engaging enough to hold attention for 20 minutes" - "It needs to be simple enough for anyone on the team to implement"

Success context gives AI a target to aim for—and helps you evaluate whether it hit that target.

> **TRY THIS**
>
> Take an AI request you recently made (or would make). Write out: - **Role:** Who are you in this context? - **Task:** What are you actually trying to accomplish? - **Constraints:** What limits apply? - **Background:** What relevant history exists? - **Success:** How will you know if the result is good?
>
> Now imagine giving AI this context before making your request.

Building Context Progressively

You don't have to dump all context upfront. In fact, building context through conversation often works better.

My security briefing preparation started with a simple statement: "I need to present our security posture to the board next week." As the conversation developed, I added layers—what the board already knew, what had changed since last quarter, which metrics would resonate with this particular group of directors, what investment I was building toward. Each exchange sharpened the AI's understanding of what I actually needed.

The progressive approach:

Opening: Establish the basics. "I'm working on a project for my team. Before I get into details, I need help thinking through the approach."

Early exchange: Add context in response to AI's initial reactions. "Good point about timelines. Our deadline is actually quite tight—two weeks. And the team is small, just three people."

Mid-conversation: Refine based on what's working and what isn't.

"Your suggestions are helpful, but I should mention—we've tried automation before and it created more problems than it solved. Let's focus on simpler approaches."

As needed: Add context when gaps become apparent. "I realize I didn't mention that this needs approval from finance. What would change about your recommendation?"

This approach has several advantages: - You don't have to guess what context will matter - You can see how AI responds and adjust - Context stays fresh and relevant rather than buried in a long opening

There's also a shortcut: ask AI what it needs to know. "I need help with a board presentation on our Q4 results. Before I give you details, what information would help you give me the best result?" Then provide answers to those questions. Let AI tell you what context matters rather than guessing.

The Cost of Missing Context

What happens when you don't provide context? Usually one of these scenarios:

Generic results. AI gives you something that could work for anyone in a roughly similar situation. You spend more time adapting it than you would have spent providing context.

Wrong assumptions. AI fills gaps with reasonable but incorrect guesses. The result looks right but misses the mark in ways you have to identify and correct.

Irrelevant suggestions. AI suggests solutions that don't work for your specific constraints. You have to reject them and try again.

Off-tone responses. AI uses a register that doesn't fit your context—too formal, too casual, too technical, too simple. The content might be fine, but the delivery is wrong.

Repeated corrections. You spend multiple exchanges correcting misunderstandings that wouldn't have happened with better initial context. The conversation becomes inefficient.

The time spent providing context is almost always less than the time spent dealing with context gaps.

Context That Often Gets Missed

Even people who understand context importance often miss these:

Audience information. Who will ultimately see or use what you're creating? Their knowledge level, preferences, and needs shape everything. A security briefing for a board of directors requires completely different framing than the same information for a technical team.

Emotional stakes. Is this a routine task or does it matter deeply to you or others? AI doesn't sense when something is sensitive unless you say so.

Your current state. Are you overwhelmed? Confused? Uncertain about direction? This affects what kind of help is most useful. Sometimes the most valuable thing AI can do isn't answer your question—it's help you figure out what the right question is.

What you've already rejected. If you've tried approaches that didn't work, AI should know—otherwise it might suggest the same things.

Cultural or organizational context. Norms that shape what's appropriate in your specific environment.

The ask behind the ask. Sometimes what you're asking for isn't what you actually need. If you're uncertain about your direction, saying so allows AI to help you clarify. My briefing preparation wasn't really about writing—it was about thinking. Once I gave AI that context, the conversation became genuinely useful.

Common Context Mistakes

Too little context: The most common problem. Results in generic outputs that require extensive revision.

Too much irrelevant context: Providing extensive background that doesn't help with the specific task. This can actually hurt by burying the relevant information.

Conflicting context: Providing signals that point in different directions. "I need something quick and simple—here's my comprehensive 50-item requirements list."

Outdated context: Using context from earlier in a conversation that's no longer accurate. If circumstances change, update the context.

Assumed shared context: Thinking AI knows something because it's obvious to you. Remember—your brilliant but inexperienced colleague (Chapter 3) wasn't in last week's meeting. AI doesn't know your company's culture, your relationship history with a client, or what happened yesterday.

Context at the wrong time: Providing crucial context after AI has already done significant work in the wrong direction. Important context should come early.

Context That Persists

Everything so far has been about single conversations. But here's what I discovered through months of working with AI across multiple projects: the real power isn't session context. It's *persistent* context—information that accumulates and carries forward.

This happened partially by design and partially by accident. As I realized that context made one project genuinely useful, I began running into the same problems across multiple projects. I'd want to use the same approaches across different projects. I had a website that supported my app, but each project existed in isolation—one didn't know anything about the other. Each new session started from zero, and I'd spend the first thirty minutes re-explaining things the AI had already understood yesterday.

So I started building context systems—files that captured the important decisions, the project architecture, the coding standards, the lessons learned. When I connected projects logically through shared context and memory files, the productivity gains were staggering. What used to take me a hundred hours, I could now do in three. That's not an exaggeration—it's the difference between an AI that understands your world and one that's meeting you for the first time every session.

This mattered enormously because I don't have unlimited time. Between my day job, my other responsibilities, and everything else competing for my attention, I might have a few hours a week for personal projects. Without persistent context, those few hours would be spent re-establishing what AI already knew. With it, I could pick up exactly where I left off and make real progress.

Our developer pilot confirmed this at scale. One key lesson: teams who created reference documents—files capturing their standards, requirements, and key decisions—got compounding returns over time. These files evolved over months as teams learned what worked. New sessions started with accumulated wisdom instead of a blank slate.

What persistent context looks like in practice:

Standards and conventions. Document how things should be done—writing style, brand voice, quality expectations, team practices. Share these at the start of every session so AI doesn't have to rediscover your preferences.

Project structure. Capture how the pieces fit together—which parts connect to which, what the workflow looks like, where the boundaries are. Without this, AI treats every question as isolated when it's actually part of a larger whole.

Decision history. Record not just what you decided but why. "We chose approach X because Y didn't work due to Z" prevents AI from enthusiastically suggesting Z in a future session.

Session handoffs. At the end of a work session, capture what was accomplished, what's next, and what the current state is. The next session starts with that context instead of starting over.

> **KEY POINT**
>
> Single-session context improves individual interactions. Persistent context compounds over time, making every future interaction better.

Context as a Skill

Providing good context gets easier the more you do it. Over time, you develop intuition for what a task needs, what assumptions AI tends to make, and how much context is enough without being excessive. You start noticing when results go sideways and can usually trace it back to a context gap.

I've come to think about context the way I think about human memory. We don't remember every detail of our lives—I couldn't tell you what I had for breakfast every day when I was seven years old. But I know I ate a lot of Cheerios and Wheaties. Our memories retain the important patterns and prune the noise. We remember enough to navigate the world effectively without being overwhelmed by every gory detail.

Context for AI works the same way. You don't need a complete history of every decision, every conversation, every iteration. You need enough accumulated context—the key patterns, the important decisions, the lessons that actually matter—for AI to provide reasonable results. Not every breakfast. Just the fact that you were a Cheerios kid.

The return on this investment is significant. Better context means better results, fewer corrections, and less time spent wrestling with AI to get what you actually need. And unlike most skills, the investment compounds. The context you build today makes tomorrow's work better. The patterns you document this month save you time next month. The standards you capture once serve you indefinitely.

> **THINK ABOUT IT**
>
> Think about the last time someone gave you a task with insufficient context—maybe a vague email from a boss or a confusing request from a client. How did you handle it? You probably asked clarifying questions. AI can't do that unless you invite it to. What would change if you started every AI interaction with the same context you'd give a new team member—and then made that context persist so you never had to give it again?

Chapter Summary

Key takeaways:

- Context is the single biggest factor in AI result quality—the AI isn't the variable, you are
- Five types of context matter most: role, task, constraints, background, and success criteria
- Context can be provided upfront or built progressively through conversation
- Persistent context—standards, architecture, decisions, session handoffs—compounds over time
- Think of context like human memory: retain the important patterns, prune the noise
- The developers who invested in context and requirements got dramatically better results than those who jumped straight to work

What's next: Chapter 6 covers the communication side of AI work—how to express what you need clearly, handle AI mistakes, and build productive back-and-forth patterns.

"Context doesn't just make AI smarter. It makes the conversation between you and AI possible in the first place."

Chapter 6: Effective AI Communication

Even after I'd learned to provide context and treat AI as a partner, something still wasn't clicking. My AI conversations felt clunky—like talking to someone who spoke a different language, requiring constant translation.

Then I watched a colleague work with AI and saw the difference immediately. She didn't just ask questions; she conversed. She gave feedback like "That's close, but more casual." She asked follow-ups like "What if we tried it from the customer's perspective?" She treated AI mistakes as information, not failure.

Here's what I realized: knowing what to tell AI wasn't enough. I needed to learn *how* to communicate with it—the rhythm of productive interaction, the art of feedback, the skill of iteration.

> **CHAPTER OVERVIEW**
>
> **What you'll learn:** - How to structure effective AI requests - The difference between commands and conversation - When to be specific versus when to let AI explore - How to handle AI mistakes productively
>
> **Why it matters:** Good communication with AI is a skill that dramatically improves your results.
>
> **Reading time:** About 12 minutes

Beyond "Prompting"

Here's a communication failure that taught me more than any success. I was helping a friend navigate a legal situation—a case where the first attorney they'd consulted had declined to take it. I asked AI to help me think through how to approach a second attorney.

The AI did what AI does: it analyzed the situation based on statistical patterns. It assumed the first attorney's rejection meant the case was weak on its merits, and it calibrated its entire approach around overcoming that perceived weakness. The suggested framing, the talking points, the strategy—all oriented around a problem that didn't actually exist.

What the AI didn't know, because I hadn't been explicit enough, was that the first attorney had declined for *market fit* reasons—it simply wasn't the type of case their firm handled. The case itself was strong. The AI had no way to know this from the information I'd provided. It filled the gap with the most statistically probable interpretation: attorney declines case, therefore case is weak.

I had to stop, synthesize everything I actually understood about the situation, and tell the AI: "Here is what I'm thinking, here is why the first rejection doesn't indicate weakness, and here is the specific angle I want to develop." Only then did the conversation become productive.

The word "prompt" has become the default term for communicating with AI. But it carries unfortunate baggage—implying that success comes from finding the magic words, the perfect incantation that unlocks the right response.

This framing is misleading. Effective AI communication isn't about prompts; it's about conversation—and about ensuring your conversation partner has the right context, not just the right question.

The prompt mindset: - Find the right words - Get the answer - If wrong, find different right words - Success is a single perfect request

The conversation mindset: - Start a dialogue - Build understanding together - Refine through iteration - Success is a productive exchange

You're not programming a computer with prompts. You're communicating with a capable assistant that can understand context, respond to feedback, and improve through iteration.

This shift in mindset changes everything.

> **KEY POINT**
>
> Stop looking for the perfect prompt. Start having better conversations.

The Anatomy of Good Requests

While conversation is the goal, individual requests still matter. Here's what makes a request effective:

Clear intent. The AI should understand what you're trying to accomplish, not just what you're asking for. "Help me explain this concept" is different from "Write a definition for this term"—and AI should know which you mean.

Appropriate specificity. Enough detail that AI understands the constraints; not so much that you've eliminated room for AI to contribute judgment. "Write exactly 237 words in the following specific format" leaves no room for AI expertise.

Success criteria when relevant. For non-trivial tasks, give AI a sense of what good looks like. "Something I could send to clients without major revision" tells AI the standard to aim for.

Openness to dialogue. Leave room for AI to ask questions, push back, or suggest alternatives. "Let me know if you need more information" signals you're open to iteration.

Honest uncertainty. If you're not sure what you need, say so. "I'm not sure if this should be a blog post or an email—what would you recommend?" allows AI to help you figure out direction.

When to Be Specific, When to Be Open

Different situations call for different communication styles.

Be specific when: - You know exactly what you want - Compliance matters (legal, regulatory, style guide) - Consistency is important (following established patterns) - You've tried open approaches and need to narrow down - The task is routine and well-understood

Specific request example: "Rewrite this paragraph to be under 100 words. Maintain the same key points but use simpler vocabulary appropriate for a general audience."

Be open when: - You're exploring options - You want AI's creative input - You're not sure what the best approach is - The task benefits from fresh perspective - You're early in the process

Open request example: "I need to communicate this change to our team. What are some approaches we could take? I'm open to formats beyond email if you think something else would work better."

Most effective communication moves between these modes—starting open to explore possibilities, then getting specific as direction becomes clear.

TRY THIS

Take a task you're working on. First, write a highly specific request for AI. Then, write a highly open request for the same task. Consider: which would produce a better result at this stage? How might you combine elements of both?

The Feedback Loop

Early on, I treated AI like a vending machine—put in a request, get back a result, decide if I liked it. If I didn't, I'd start over with a completely new request. It took me embarrassingly long to realize I could just *tell the AI what was wrong*.

"That's too formal." "The second paragraph is stronger than the first—build on that." "You're missing the main point, which is..." These kinds of responses felt strange at first—like giving performance feedback to a toaster. But the difference in output quality was immediate and dramatic.

Feedback is how AI interactions improve. Yet most people give minimal feedback or none at all—accepting whatever comes back or starting over entirely.

Types of useful feedback:

Direction adjustments. "Good start, but I need it more formal." "This covers the main points, but let's add more detail on the budget section."

Specific corrections. "The tone is right, but these numbers are wrong—the actual figures are..." "Great structure, but we should mention the deadline in the opening."

Priority clarification. "You've covered a lot of ground, but the key message is getting lost. Let's focus on the three main benefits and cut the rest."

Positive reinforcement. "That's exactly what I was looking for—the conclusion is particularly strong." This helps AI understand what's working.

Confusion signals. "I'm not sure this is going in the right direction. Can we step back and talk about the overall approach?"

Feedback doesn't need to be elaborate. Even simple signals—"too long," "more casual," "closer"—help AI calibrate.

Handling Mistakes

AI makes mistakes. This isn't a failure of the technology—it's the nature of working with any collaborator. The question is how you respond.

I had a maddening experience with this while working on a book project. I'd gone through extensive revisions of a cover design, working through multiple versions with AI assistance—generating visuals, iterating on text layouts, refining the composition. At one point, I'd explored a fifth version of the cover that I ultimately discarded, deciding the fourth version was stronger.

But the AI latched onto that discarded fifth version. In subsequent conversations about the book, it kept referencing "the v5 cover"—making suggestions based on a design I'd abandoned. I corrected it. It found other references to v5 in our working files. I told it to delete those. It did. But the next conversation, there it was again—the AI pulling from cached context and pattern-matching to the wrong version.

The fix wasn't a single correction. I had to systematically update every context file, every memory reference, every working document to explicitly state: "v4 is the authoritative cover. There is no v5." Only when the *entire context* was consistent did the AI stop resurrecting the discarded version.

The lesson? AI doesn't just make one-off mistakes. It can systematically latch onto the wrong pattern if your working context contains contradictory signals. Fixing the output isn't enough—sometimes you have to fix the inputs that are leading AI astray.

Unhelpful responses to mistakes: - Getting frustrated - Starting over completely - Blaming the tool - Giving up on the task

Helpful responses to mistakes:

Identify the type of mistake. Was it a context gap (AI didn't know something it needed)? A wrong assumption (AI guessed incorrectly)? A capability limit (AI can't do this type of task well)? A contaminated context (AI is drawing from outdated or contradictory information)? The response differs by type.

Provide correction, not just rejection. "That's not quite right" gives AI nothing to work with. "The tone is too formal—we have a casual relationship with this client" gives direction.

Ask what went wrong. "What led you to that conclusion?" or "What assumptions are you making about my situation?" can reveal gaps you didn't know existed.

Adjust your approach if needed. If the same type of mistake keeps happening, the problem might be in how you're communicating, not in the AI. With my cover design issue, the AI wasn't malfunctioning—it was faithfully following signals I hadn't cleaned up.

Know when to pivot. Sometimes a line of conversation isn't working. It's fine to say "Let's try a different approach" rather than continuing to refine something that's fundamentally off track.

Mistakes are information. They tell you what context is missing, what assumptions need correction, or what limits exist. Used well, mistakes make subsequent interactions better.

> **KEY POINT**
>
> Treat AI mistakes as diagnostic information, not evidence of failure.

Conversation Patterns That Work

After hundreds of AI conversations—some productive, many not—I started noticing patterns. Not in what I was asking about, but in *how* the conversations flowed when they worked well. The productive interactions shared recognizable shapes. The frustrating ones did too, which made them avoidable once I could name them.

These patterns are specific ways to implement the plan-execute-verify loop from Chapter 4. Here are several that consistently produce good results:

The exploration pattern. Start broad, narrow progressively. “What are the main approaches to [problem]?” □ “Let’s focus on approach B. What would implementation look like?” □ “Great, now help me draft the first section.”

The refinement pattern. Generate, then improve. This is the pattern I use most. You saw it in Chapter 4 with the board presentation—starting broad, incorporating my boss’s feedback, iterating until fifteen pages became six. The refinement pattern is what made that collaboration work.

The pattern looks like: “Give me a rough draft” □ “The structure is good, but the opening is weak—make it more engaging” □ “Better. Now strengthen the call to action.” Each pass gets closer to what you need.

The rubber duck pattern. Think out loud, get reactions. “I’m thinking about this problem. Here’s where I am... [explain your thinking]. What am I missing?” AI can spot gaps, suggest alternatives, or confirm your direction.

The stress-test pattern. Challenge your own ideas. “I’m planning to [approach]. What could go wrong? Play devil’s advocate.” AI can identify weaknesses you might miss.

The expansion pattern. Build from a seed. “Here’s my core idea: [idea]. Help me develop this into a full proposal, identifying what sections we need and what questions need answering.”

The translation pattern. Transform between contexts. “I have this technical explanation. Help me rewrite it for a non-technical board presentation" or "I drafted this informally—now make it appropriate for a formal report."

Communication Calibration

This is the part that can't be taught from a book—only learned through practice. I can name the variables, but the feel for them develops through doing. Over time, you learn to calibrate your communication to different situations:

Task complexity. Simple tasks need less setup. Complex tasks benefit from more back-and-forth before diving in.

Importance. High-stakes work warrants more careful communication and verification. Low-stakes work can be faster and less precise.

Your clarity. When you know exactly what you want, be direct. When you're uncertain, invite exploration.

AI's track record. With tasks AI does well, you can communicate more loosely. With tasks AI often struggles with, more specific guidance helps.

Time available. When you have time, longer conversations produce better results. When pressed, efficient communication matters.

Pay attention to what works, and your instincts will sharpen.

Common Communication Pitfalls

I've made every one of these mistakes. Some of them repeatedly. Naming them helped me stop—or at least catch myself faster.

The interrogation. Treating AI like a witness rather than a collaborator. Rapid-fire questions without building understanding.

The monologue. Providing extensive context but no invitation for AI to respond, ask questions, or contribute.

The vague request. "Make it better" without any indication of what "better" means in this context.

The one-shot. Putting all hope in a single request rather than expecting iteration.

The impatient restart. Abandoning a productive conversation because the first response wasn't perfect.

The over-correction. Responding to one mistake by swinging too far in the opposite direction.

Building Communication Skills

In my experience, the biggest leaps in AI communication come from paying attention to what's working—and what isn't. Here's how to accelerate that learning:

Vary your approaches. Try different communication styles with similar tasks. Notice what produces better results.

Learn from friction. When an interaction feels difficult, analyze why. The friction often points to communication patterns you can improve.

Borrow from human communication. Clarity, feedback, active listening, and adjusting to your conversational partner—these principles apply to AI as much as to people.

> **THINK ABOUT IT**
>
> Think about the best communicator you know—someone who always seems to get what they need from others. What makes them effective? Chances are, they're clear about what they want, they listen to responses, and they adjust course based on feedback. These same skills make someone effective with AI.

Chapter Summary

Key takeaways:

- Effective AI interaction is conversation, not one-shot prompting
- Different situations call for different communication styles—sometimes specific, sometimes open
- Feedback is how AI interactions improve; give it consistently
- Treat mistakes as diagnostic information that improves future interactions
- Communication skill develops through attention to what works and willingness to adjust

What's next: Part 3 puts these principles into practice across specific use cases—writing, research, decision-making, and personal productivity.

"The question isn't 'What's the right prompt?' but 'How do we work toward the right result together?'"

Chapter 7: AI for Writing and Communication

I had twenty minutes before a board presentation draft was due. I knew exactly what I wanted to say—the strategy was clear in my head—but the blank document just sat there. The cursor blinked. I typed a sentence, deleted it, typed another. Five minutes gone with nothing to show for it.

So I opened my AI assistant and described the situation: the strategic pivot we were recommending, the board members who'd resist, the data that supported our position, the tone I needed. Fifteen minutes later, I had a solid draft. Not perfect—I'd rewritten the opening, sharpened the financial arguments, and completely changed the conclusion. But I'd gone from blank page to something I could defend in the time I used to spend just organizing my thoughts.

That experience taught me something I keep coming back to: AI's biggest writing contribution isn't the words it generates. It's breaking the paralysis of the blank page. This chapter is about that transformation—using AI to accelerate your writing without losing your voice or your judgment.

CHAPTER OVERVIEW

What you'll learn: - How to use AI for different types of writing - Techniques for maintaining your authentic voice -

When AI helps most and when to write yourself - Practical workflows for common writing tasks

Why it matters: Writing is how most knowledge work gets communicated. AI can dramatically accelerate it.

Reading time: About 12 minutes

The Blank Page Problem

Most writing difficulty isn't about writing—it's about starting. The blank page presents infinite possibilities, and infinite possibilities create paralysis.

AI solves this problem elegantly. Instead of staring at blankness, you can: - Ask AI to create an outline based on your key points - Request a rough first draft you can react to - Generate multiple opening approaches to choose from - Have AI ask questions that help you clarify your thinking

The shift is profound—instead of creating from nothing, you're editing and refining something. That's psychologically easier and often produces better results faster.

But there's a trap. If you accept AI's first draft wholesale, your writing becomes generic—competent but forgettable. The real skill is using AI to overcome the blank page while keeping your distinctive voice and judgment.

KEY POINT

AI's greatest writing value is often getting you past the blank page. What you do after that determines whether the result is yours or generic.

Email and Professional Communication

Start with the writing most of us do most often: email and workplace messages.

I used to spend half an hour crafting emails that didn't warrant half an hour—a status update to my leadership team, a meeting follow-up with action items, a polite decline of a vendor pitch. None of these required my best prose. They required accuracy, appropriate tone, and speed. These were the first writing tasks I handed to AI, and the time savings alone justified the experiment. But I also learned where the line is: the email to a board member about a sensitive governance issue? That one I write myself.

AI excels at:

Drafting routine communications. Meeting requests, status updates, standard responses—AI can produce these quickly and competently. You review for accuracy and send.

Adjusting tone. "Make this more formal" or "soften this without losing the key message" are requests AI handles well. You know what you want to say; AI helps you say it appropriately.

Handling difficult messages. Need to deliver bad news? Push back on a request? Navigate a sensitive situation? AI can offer multiple approaches and help you find language that's firm but not inflammatory.

Summarizing and responding. Long email threads you need to catch up on? AI can summarize the discussion and draft a response that addresses the key points.

Practical workflow for email:

1. **Quick emails:** Describe what you need to communicate, let AI draft, review and send
2. **Important emails:** Draft yourself, ask AI to review for tone and clarity, revise based on feedback

3. **Difficult emails:** Ask AI for multiple approaches, choose elements from each, craft your response

TRY THIS

Take an email you've been putting off writing. Instead of drafting it yourself, describe the situation to AI: who you're writing to, what you need to communicate, what tone is appropriate, and any sensitivities to navigate. Review what AI produces. How does it compare to what you would have written? What would you change?

Reports, Proposals, and Documents

Longer documents require more sophisticated AI collaboration. This is where the investment in context from Chapter 5 really pays off.

I recently used AI to help produce a 250-page analytical methodology document. The AI didn't write it—I iterated through every section, providing my analysis and judgment, while AI helped me structure arguments and maintain consistency across a document too large to hold in my head all at once. The result was something I couldn't have produced as quickly alone, but it was unmistakably my thinking. That's the right balance for serious documents.

For proposals:

Start by giving AI the full context: what you're proposing, who will read it, what concerns they're likely to have, and what would make them say yes. Ask AI to create a structure before drafting content. Review the structure first—it's easier to fix a bad outline than a bad draft.

Then work section by section. AI drafts; you review, refine, and add specifics only you know. Pay particular attention to sections where you're making the case—these need your voice and judgment, not generic persuasion.

For reports:

AI shines at report writing because reports often follow predictable structures. Give AI your data, your conclusions, and your audience, and it can produce a solid framework.

But beware: AI will happily produce reports that sound authoritative while saying very little. Always ask yourself: Does this report actually tell the reader something useful? Does it make clear recommendations? Is it specific to our situation?

For documentation:

Procedures, guides, how-to documents—these are excellent AI territory. The content tends to be straightforward; the challenge is making it clear and complete. AI is good at both.

Workflow: Create a rough outline of what needs to be covered. Have AI expand each section. Review for accuracy and completeness. Have someone unfamiliar with the topic review for clarity.

Creative and Personal Writing

Here's where things get interesting—and where AI assistance requires the most care.

AI can help with creative writing, but the nature of the help changes. For professional writing, AI can often produce a solid first draft. For creative writing, AI's drafts tend toward the generic, the expected, the cliche. I've seen it firsthand—ask AI to write something "creative" and you'll get something that reads like every other piece of AI-generated content. Technically correct, emotionally flat.

Where AI helps with creative work:

Brainstorming and ideation. "Give me ten different ways this story could begin" or "What are some unexpected directions this character could take?" AI generates options; you choose what resonates.

Overcoming blocks. When you're stuck, having AI write *some-*

thing—even something you'll mostly discard—can restart your creative flow.

Mechanics and polish. Once you've written something you like, AI can help with grammar, clarity, and flow without changing your voice.

Research and details. Writing about a setting you don't know well? AI can provide details that make your writing more vivid and accurate.

Where AI doesn't help with creative work:

Original voice. AI writes in patterns. Your distinctive voice comes from breaking patterns in your own way. Let AI help with mechanics; protect your voice.

Emotional truth. The moments that make creative writing powerful—genuine emotion, hard-won insight, authentic perspective—don't come from pattern-matching.

Real creativity. AI combines existing patterns in new ways. Genuine creative breakthroughs come from human imagination seeing possibilities AI wouldn't conceive.

> **THINK ABOUT IT**
>
> Consider something you've written that you're proud of. What makes it distinctively yours? Could AI have produced it? Understanding what makes your writing valuable helps you know what to protect when using AI.

Maintaining Your Voice

The most common concern about AI writing assistance: "Will everything I write start sounding the same—generic, AI-ish?"

It's a legitimate concern, and I'll be honest—it's one I've wrestled with while writing this book. AI naturally gravitates toward average, middle-of-the-road language. Without active resistance, AI-assisted writing becomes bland. Safe. Forgettable.

Techniques for maintaining your voice:

Write first, AI second. For important pieces, write your first draft yourself. Then use AI for refinement, expansion, or polish. Your voice stays primary.

Edit aggressively. Don't accept AI's word choices automatically. If a phrase doesn't sound like you, change it. Your voice lives in specific word choices, sentence rhythms, and ways of framing ideas.

Provide examples. Give AI samples of your previous writing and ask it to match the style. This won't be perfect, but it helps AI understand your patterns.

Use AI for structure, yourself for substance. Let AI organize your ideas and provide frameworks. Write the actual content—especially anything that expresses opinions, shares experiences, or makes arguments—yourself.

Review with fresh eyes. After incorporating AI assistance, read the whole piece aloud. Does it sound like you? Where does it feel generic? Revise those spots.

When to Write Without AI

Not everything benefits from AI assistance. Knowing when to write alone is part of the skill.

Write yourself when:

The message is deeply personal. Condolences, congratulations, expressions of genuine appreciation—these should come from you, with all their imperfections.

Your authentic voice is the point. Thought leadership, personal essays, anything where readers come for your perspective—AI assistance can dilute what makes it valuable.

You're thinking through something. Sometimes writing is how you figure out what you think. AI shortcuts this process in ways that prevent genuine insight.

The relationship matters. Messages to close colleagues, important clients, or anyone who knows you well should sound like you. They'll notice if they don't.

You're learning. If you're developing a skill—persuasive writing, technical communication, creative expression—doing the work yourself builds capability that AI assistance doesn't.

Practical Workflows by Task

What follows are the workflows I've settled on after months of experimentation. They're not the only way—but they represent what I've found actually works in practice, not just in theory. Adapt them to your own patterns.

Quick professional email: 1. Think: What's the core message? What action do I want? 2. AI: "Draft an email to [recipient] about [topic]. Key points: [list]. Tone: [professional/friendly/formal]." 3. Review: Check accuracy, adjust tone, send. Time: 2-5 minutes.

Important email or message: 1. Draft the key points yourself 2. AI: "Expand this into a complete email. Make it [more formal/softer/clearer]." 3. Review closely: Does it say what I mean? Is the tone right? 4. Revise and send. Time: 10-15 minutes.

Report or analysis: 1. Gather your data and conclusions 2. AI: "Create an outline for a report on [topic] for [audience]. Include: [sections]." 3. Review outline, adjust structure 4. AI: Draft each section based on your data and points 5. Heavy review: Add specifics, fix inaccuracies, ensure recommendations are clear 6. Final polish. Time: Varies by length; typically 30-50% faster than writing from scratch.

Proposal: 1. Define: What am I proposing? To whom? What objections will they have? 2. AI: "Suggest a structure for a proposal to [do

X] for [audience]. Address concerns about [Y]." 3. Refine structure 4. Draft each section with AI, adding your specifics 5. Pay special attention to the "why" sections—these need your voice 6. Final review: Does this actually persuade? Is it specific enough? Time: Varies; significant time saved on structure and drafting.

Thought piece or personal writing: 1. Write your first draft yourself 2. AI: "Review this for clarity and flow. Suggest improvements without changing my voice." 3. Selectively incorporate suggestions 4. Read aloud, revise what doesn't sound like you. Time: AI speeds polish, not creation.

KEY POINT

The right workflow depends on the type of writing and how much your distinctive voice matters. Adjust AI involvement accordingly.

Common Mistakes

I've made all of these. The first one cost me—I sent a report to a colleague that read fine but had none of my usual directness. She noticed. "Did you write this?" she asked. I had, technically. But I'd let AI smooth away everything distinctive about how I communicate. That was the wake-up call.

Over-reliance on AI drafts. If you always accept AI's first draft with minor tweaks, your writing becomes generic. Push back, rewrite, make it yours.

Under-specifying context. "Write an email about the project" produces generic results. "Write an email to my skeptical manager requesting a timeline extension because the vendor delayed delivery" produces useful results.

Skipping review for "quick" messages. Even quick messages benefit from a read-through. AI makes mistakes, and you own what you send.

Using AI for everything. Some messages should be yours alone. Know which ones.

Forgetting the audience. AI writes for a generic reader. You know your specific audience. Make sure the final product fits them.

Chapter Summary

Key takeaways:

- AI's greatest writing value is overcoming the blank page—providing structure and drafts to react to
- Different writing tasks call for different levels of AI involvement
- Maintaining your voice requires active editing, not passive acceptance of AI output
- Some writing should remain entirely yours—personal messages, authentic voice pieces, learning opportunities
- The right workflow matches AI involvement to the task and the importance of your distinctive voice

What's next: Chapter 8 explores how AI can accelerate research and learning—helping you understand new topics, find information, and develop expertise faster.

"AI can get you past the blank page. What you do after that—the rewrites, the sharpening, the moments where you say 'no, that's not what I mean'—that's where your writing lives."

Chapter 8: AI for Research and Analysis

My first serious AI research project wasn't an article or a report. It was a comprehensive corporate analysis—the kind of board-level strategic assessment that covers everything from financial performance and governance structure to competitive positioning, regulatory risk, and activist investor vulnerability. The company was CoreCivic, and I wanted to understand it deeply enough to brief a board of directors.

Traditionally, this kind of analysis takes a team of analysts weeks or months. You read the 10-K filings, pull apart the proxy statements, review press releases, study analyst reports, cross-reference SEC data, and synthesize it all into a coherent narrative. I'd done variations of this work throughout my career. I knew what good looked like.

With AI as my research partner, I produced a comprehensive analysis that ran to hundreds of pages across twenty sections—company overview, financial analysis, governance assessment, competitive positioning, risk evaluation, and more. The timeline compressed from months to weeks. Not because AI did the thinking, but because it accelerated everything that fed my thinking: the reading, the synthesis, the first-draft structuring, the identification of patterns across disparate data sources. I could explore a question about debt covenants, pivot to executive compensation benchmarking, and circle back to supply chain risk without losing my thread.

But this project also taught me—sometimes painfully—where AI research breaks down and where human judgment remains irreplaceable.

This chapter is about what I learned: how to use AI as a research and analysis partner, how to verify what it gives you, and how to build a methodology that produces genuinely reliable results.

CHAPTER OVERVIEW

What you'll learn: - How to use AI for effective research and information gathering - Techniques for analysis and synthesis of complex topics - Critical verification practices for factual claims - How to build knowledge progressively with AI assistance

Why it matters: Research capability determines the quality of decisions, strategies, and understanding.

Reading time: About 15 minutes

The 80/20 Flip

Before diving into methodology, I want to share the insight that reframed how I think about AI-assisted research entirely.

I'd been discussing my corporate analysis work with my Chase investment advisor—we talk frequently about AI and which investments make sense in this space. When I showed him the comprehensive analysis I'd produced, he was impressed enough to want to share it internally. It turns out Chase has been building its own analytics capabilities to reduce reliance on proxy advisory firms like Glass Lewis and ISS—companies that provide corporate governance assessments to institutional investors.

We ended up in a conversation about what AI actually changes about research, and he crystallized something I'd been feeling but hadn't articulated: traditionally, professionals spend about eighty percent of their time on research and data collection, leaving only twenty percent for the analysis and meaning-making that actually creates value. AI flips that ratio. You spend twenty percent of your time on research—AI handles the data gathering, the synthesis, the first-pass structuring—and eighty percent on the analysis, the interpretation, the creation of genuine insight.

That's the real promise of AI-assisted research. Not that AI replaces your thinking. That it frees you to spend the vast majority of your time on what actually matters: figuring out what the data means, why it matters, and what to do about it.

Every technique in this chapter serves that flip. The goal isn't just to get AI to research faster. It's to reclaim your time for the work that only you can do.

AI as Research Partner

A colleague once watched me walk through the materials I'd produced for a board-level analysis—the comprehensive report, the activist investor briefing, a facilitation guide, a complete tabletop exercise with injects and scenarios. He asked where I'd pulled all those documents from.

"I made them," I said.

His jaw dropped. "With your AI widget?"

The conversation that followed lasted half an hour. He couldn't believe that the volume and quality of research artifacts had come from one person working with AI. But the most important part of that conversation wasn't about AI's capabilities—it was about what AI *couldn't* do, and why the documents were good despite that.

Think of AI as an incredibly well-read research assistant who has access to vast information but lacks your specific context and judgment.

This assistant can: - Summarize complex topics quickly - Explain concepts at varying levels of depth - Identify key arguments and counterarguments - Synthesize information from multiple angles - Answer follow-up questions instantly

This assistant cannot: - Access real-time information (unless connected to search) - Verify its own accuracy - Know which specific sources you'd trust - Replace domain expertise you don't have - Guarantee that confident-sounding answers are correct

Understanding both capabilities and limitations is essential for effective research collaboration. My colleague was impressed by the output, but it was only as good as the judgment I applied to every piece of data AI retrieved.

> **KEY POINT**
>
> AI is a powerful research accelerator, not a replacement for judgment. Use it to gather and synthesize; verify and evaluate yourself.

Starting Research: The Right Foundation

When I began the CoreCivic analysis, I didn't start by asking AI to "tell me about CoreCivic." That would have produced a generic Wikipedia-style overview—accurate in broad strokes but useless for board-level work.

Instead, I started with a ninety-page document from a governance education program that outlined every dimension a comprehensive corporate analysis should cover: financial health metrics, governance structure evaluation, regulatory exposure, competitive positioning frameworks, and dozens of specific questions a board director should be able to answer. I fed that document to AI as the foundation for a research prompt.

The difference was dramatic. Instead of getting a surface-level overview, I got a structured analysis that knew to look at debt covenant compliance, proxy statement disclosures, insider ownership patterns, and activist investor vulnerability scores. The framework told AI *what* to investigate. My expertise told me *what the results meant.*

This principle applies to any research project, not just corporate analysis. The quality of your research output is directly proportional to the quality of the foundation you give AI.

Effective approaches to starting research:

Start with what you know. Before asking AI anything, articulate what you already understand and what specifically you need to learn. "I know X, but I need to understand Y in the context of Z" produces far better results than "tell me about Y."

Give AI your framework. If you have a methodology, an outline, a set of questions, or even a rough structure for what you're investigating, share it. AI works dramatically better when it understands the shape of what you're building.

Define your audience. Research for a board of directors looks different from research for a team meeting, which looks different from research for personal learning. Tell AI who will use this information and how.

Specify your depth. "Give me an overview" and "give me a detailed analysis with supporting evidence" produce very different outputs. Be explicit about what level of depth you need.

TRY THIS

Choose a topic you've been meaning to understand better—something relevant to your work or interests that you haven't had time to explore. Before asking AI anything, spend five minutes writing down: What do I already know? What specifically do I need to learn? Who is this for? Then use those answers as the foundation for your first AI research conversation. Notice how this preparation changes the quality of what you receive.

Going Deeper: The Art of the Prompt

Once you have the landscape, you can investigate specific areas more deeply. But I learned something important as my research projects grew more ambitious: the most effective approach isn't to ask AI your question directly. It's to ask AI to *help you build the right prompt* for your question.

My early research prompts were a few pages long. As I refined my methodology, they grew to twenty pages, then fifty, then over a hundred. I described the output I wanted, the input I thought was relevant, who my audience was, what I was looking to get out of the analysis, and how I wanted to analyze the results myself. I added supporting documentation, research methodology, and reference materials. Then I asked AI to produce a comprehensive research prompt from all of that context.

A colleague once reacted to this: "I used to just type two sentences—'Hi, can you please research this?' And you're giving the AI tool *fifteen pages*?"

"Yeah," I said. "And I'm using it to give me a prompt before I even start. I'm asking it to help me build the prompt."

That's the difference between getting a generic answer and getting a genuinely useful one. The investment in prompt design pays back exponentially in output quality.

Techniques for deeper exploration:

Progressive depth. Start with overviews, then ask for more detail on areas that matter. "Tell me more about [specific aspect]" or "Explain [concept] in more detail" lets you drill down where needed. In my corporate analyses, I would get the landscape first, then dive into specific sections one at a time—financial analysis, then governance, then competitive positioning—because trying to do everything at once overwhelmed the system.

Multiple perspectives. "What would critics of this approach say?" or "What's the strongest argument against this position?" ensures you're not getting a one-sided view.

Practical implications. "How would this apply to [my specific situation]?" or "What would implementation actually look like?" grounds abstract concepts in reality.

Historical context. "How did this develop? What's the history?" often reveals important nuances that pure conceptual explanations miss.

Edge cases. "Where does this break down? What are the exceptions?" identifies limitations of frameworks or approaches.

Analysis and Synthesis

Beyond gathering information, AI can help you make sense of what you've learned—but with an important caveat that I discovered during my GeneDx analysis.

After the CoreCivic project, I applied the same methodology to a comprehensive analysis of GeneDx, a genomics company. AI picked up the key strategic data. It identified their financial trajectory, their market position, their governance structure. It even applied the right business frameworks—SWOT analysis, competitive five forces, growth assessment.

But it missed the meaning.

GeneDx had recently completed an acquisition that represented a significantly different strategic approach and opportunity for the company. It was obvious to me—a seasoned professional who'd evaluated dozens of strategic pivots across industries—that this acquisition fundamentally changed their competitive position and growth trajectory. AI treated it as another data point. It applied the frameworks correctly but missed the *significance* of what the frameworks revealed.

This is the fundamental limitation I keep running into: AI does exactly what you say, not necessarily exactly what you want. It will give you a view of the data that may seem nuanced—and in some cases there is some nuance—but it's often one-dimensional. AI identifies the correlations, applies the right labels, and produces structurally correct analysis. But to truly extract value, you need human guidelines, human analytics, human meaning-making, and human judgment added to the mix.

The GeneDx experience was strangely comforting. AI could accelerate my learning, help me pull together the data, and give me a solid first layer of business analysis. But it really took human expertise to pull out truly meaningful observations and develop a genuinely competitive strategic assessment. The pattern recognition was AI's job. The meaning-making was mine.

This is the essential partnership in AI-assisted analysis—and it's why the 80/20 flip matters so much. You don't want to spend eighty percent of your time gathering data that AI can gather in minutes. You want to spend eighty percent of your time on what AI can't do: recognizing what's truly significant, connecting patterns across your experience, and creating genuine insight.

AI excels at: Synthesizing large volumes of data, applying standard analytical frameworks, identifying patterns across documents, and producing structured first drafts of analysis.

You provide: Domain expertise that recognizes significance, cross-industry pattern recognition, strategic judgment about what matters, and the contextual understanding that turns data into insight.

When you're working through analysis with AI, keep this division of labor in mind. Ask AI to synthesize themes, compare options, identify assumptions, and structure arguments. But apply your own judgment to questions of *significance*—what matters most, what the data actually implies for your specific situation, and what it all means for decisions you need to make.

KEY POINT

> AI knows a lot of the right business frameworks and can help with layering a first pass of analysis. But it still misses the nuances you get by personally reading the source documents, reviewing the overall sentiment, and understanding the broader context.

The Verification Imperative

Here's the uncomfortable truth about AI research—one I've learned the hard way more than once: AI will confidently present incorrect information as fact. This isn't occasional. It's inherent to how the technology works.

When I started doing analysis on large bodies of data, I got reasonably good research and detailed output. But I discovered three distinct categories of data problems.

Bad sources. Some data was pulled from outdated or unreliable sources. The internet is full of information that was accurate five years ago but isn't anymore, or that was never accurate but got widely repeated. AI doesn't distinguish between a primary SEC filing and a three-year-old blog post summarizing what someone else said about that filing. Using a high-quality AI model reduced hallucination almost to zero, but there's a lot of bad data publicly available, and AI will retrieve it confidently.

Incomplete data. All the data I asked for was obtained, but not necessarily from multiple sources. Some figures came from a single analyst report or one news article rather than being cross-referenced against corporate filings and SEC data. The varying levels of reliability were invisible in the output—everything looked equally authoritative.

The storks-and-babies problem. A few months ago, I asked AI about a German study I remembered from grad school that showed countries with more storks also had more babies. AI retrieved the information correctly. But the entire point of that study was to illustrate the difference between correlation and causation—a distinction that AI, working from pattern recognition alone, struggles with. AI can find the correlation in your data. It often can't tell you whether the correlation is meaningful, coincidental, or misleading. That kind of critical thinking requires human judgment applied across broad domains.

My verification methodology evolved through painful experience:

I started with a simple data validation prompt—essentially asking AI to flag its own uncertainty levels. That helped, but not enough.

Then I added source citation requirements at the end of each section. This helped me trace where claims originated, but unsupported assertions still slipped through.

Next, I added a human review layer—asking explicitly: What data is missing? What does this data mean? What are the limitations of AI's interpretation? This was where the real value emerged. The human interpretation of data, as it always has been, was the most important part. It took expert knowledge across industries to bring meaning and context to the analysis.

My final methodology uses a four-tier verification system:

- **Tier 1:** Primary sources—SEC filings, official corporate disclosures, regulatory databases. Highest reliability.
- **Tier 2:** Established secondary sources—major analyst reports, recognized industry research. High reliability but verify key claims.
- **Tier 3:** Third-party reporting—business journalism, industry commentary, expert analysis. Useful for perspective but cross-reference critical facts.
- **Tier 4:** General references—blog posts, social media, aggregated content. Use only for context and sentiment, never for factual claims.

This changed my process from hoping AI got things right to systematically knowing what I could trust and what required additional verification.

KEY POINT

The more confident AI sounds, the more carefully you should verify. Confidence indicates pattern-matching strength, not factual accuracy.

Building Knowledge Over Time

One of AI's limitations is that each conversation typically starts fresh—AI doesn't remember your previous research. For a quick question, this doesn't matter. For serious research that extends over days or weeks, it's a significant constraint.

I hit this wall hard. As my corporate analysis prompts grew longer and more detailed—some exceeding a hundred pages of context, reference material, and methodology—I ran into practical limits. The analysis would crash in the middle of producing the first section, or it would get three-quarters of the way through a document I was watching it produce, then everything would lock up and the work would disappear.

I learned to break my analysis into sections, having AI work through them one at a time and saving the results as I went. But even then, I was iterating through each section multiple times—asking clarifying questions, requesting additional data, probing the analysis, running verification checks, and pushing for deeper insight before moving on.

The real breakthrough came when I built a system around the research process itself. I created memory files that maintained context across the entire project—whether the research spanned minutes, hours, days, or a month. I built a structured file system where all data was automatically saved and organized for reference. And I created guidelines that instructed the system to update all context files before running out of memory, ensuring that nothing was lost even when individual sessions ended.

You don't need anything that elaborate to benefit from the same principle. The core idea is simple:

Maintain your own notes. As you learn through AI conversations, capture key points in your own documents. These become your research record and can be shared with AI in future conversations.

Create summary documents. After a research session, ask AI to summarize the key findings. Save this summary and start future conversations by sharing it: "Here's what I've learned so far..."

Build progressively. For ongoing topics, maintain a document that captures your current understanding. Update it as you learn more. Share relevant sections when starting new conversations. Your research should build like layers—each session adding to what came before rather than starting over.

Separate what AI said from what you've verified. This is critical. Keep a clear record of which claims come from AI synthesis and which you've confirmed through primary sources. When you come back to your research weeks later, you need to know what you can cite confidently and what still needs checking.

> **THINK ABOUT IT**
>
> Consider a research question you've been exploring—or want to explore—over time. How would you structure your own notes to maintain context across multiple AI conversations? What system would help you build knowledge progressively rather than starting fresh each time?

Research for Different Purposes

Different research goals require different approaches, but the same principles apply: start with a foundation, build progressively, and verify what matters.

Competitive or market research. Start with the landscape, then drill into specific competitors or market segments. Have AI apply standard analytical frameworks—but apply your own judgment to what the analysis means for your specific situation. Verify financial data and market share figures against primary sources.

Learning a new domain. Get the conceptual foundations first, then understand the vocabulary, the key debates, and what experts care about. Build progressively over multiple sessions. This is where AI's breadth is most valuable—it can give you a reasonable map of almost any field in a single conversation.

Preparing for a presentation or meeting. Research the topic and key arguments, anticipate questions and objections, and develop clear explanations for complex points. This is where the synthesis capability shines—ask AI to help you structure your thinking, identify weak points in your argument, and prepare for the hardest questions you might face.

Supporting a major decision. Understand the options and trade-offs, research how others have approached similar decisions, identify evaluation criteria, and analyze risks. Use the verification framework for any facts that will influence the decision.

When AI Isn't Enough

Some research requires more than AI conversation, and recognizing when you've hit that boundary is one of the most important research skills.

Primary sources. When you need to know exactly what someone said, what a document states, or what data shows, go to the source. In my GeneDx analysis, personally reading the 10-K filings, the press releases, and reviewing overall market sentiment revealed nuances that AI's summaries missed entirely. AI can point you toward sources and give you a head start on understanding them, but don't rely on AI's interpretation alone.

Current events. Unless your AI has real-time search capabilities, it won't know about recent developments. For current information, use traditional search or news sources. AI can help you put current events in context once you bring the information to the conversation.

Specialized expertise. AI has broad knowledge but can be shallow in specialized domains. For technical, legal, medical, or other expert questions, consult actual experts. AI can help you prepare questions and understand answers, but it's not a substitute for expertise. The political environment, regulatory mood, and interpersonal dynamics that shape business decisions exist in a context that AI doesn't have access to.

Original research. AI can help you analyze existing information but can't conduct new research—surveys, interviews, experiments, original data collection require human effort.

Avoiding Research Pitfalls

Every research pitfall on this list is one I've fallen into personally. Some of them more than once.

The confirmation trap. It's easy to use AI to confirm what you already believe. I've caught myself asking leading questions that produced exactly the analysis I expected. The fix is simple in theory, hard in practice: actively seek contradicting views. "What's the strongest argument against my position?" should be a standard part of every research session.

The depth illusion. AI can produce pages of confident-sounding analysis without much depth. Early in my corporate analysis work, I accepted some sections that looked thorough but were actually surface-level pattern matching—correct frameworks applied without genuine insight. Now I push for specifics. If AI gives me a SWOT analysis, I ask: "What's the evidence for each of these? Which ones are you most and least confident about?"

The currency mistake. AI's training has a cutoff date. For rapidly evolving topics, what AI "knows" may be outdated. I've learned to always ask when data was current and to verify anything time-sensitive against current sources.

Over-reliance. AI research is fast and easy, which can make you skip harder but more valuable research. There were times I almost didn't read a company's actual 10-K filing because AI had already "summarized" it for me. Every time I forced myself to read the primary source, I found something AI missed.

The expert illusion. AI can make you feel expert after a few conversations. But pattern-matched knowledge isn't the same as genuine expertise built through years of deep engagement with a field. After my GeneDx analysis, I showed the work to a colleague who'd spent decades in governance. His feedback was invaluable precisely because it came from experience I couldn't replicate with AI conversations.

Accepting errors as success. This is the most insidious trap: treating any AI output as acceptable simply because it exists. When you're tired or rushed, it's tempting to accept whatever AI produces—even when it hedges with "I couldn't find specific information" or generates generic content that doesn't actually answer your question.

The standard shouldn't be "AI gave me something" but "AI gave me something useful and accurate."

Evaluating AI Output Quality

Develop habits for actively evaluating what AI produces:

The substance check. Does this response contain actual information, or is it primarily hedging, generalization, and filler? A paragraph that reads "This is an important topic with many perspectives that professionals consider when making decisions" says nothing useful despite sounding reasonable.

The specificity test. Are there specific facts, examples, or data points? Or just abstract claims? Quality research produces concrete details, not just conceptual frameworks.

The answer test. Does this actually answer what I asked? It's surprisingly common for AI to produce coherent, well-structured responses that address a related question rather than your actual question.

The confidence-calibration check. Does the certainty of the language match the reliability of the content? Be especially skeptical when AI sounds maximally confident about things that are contested, uncertain, or outside its training data.

Don't settle for mediocre output when your research matters. Push for better, provide more context, or recognize that you need sources beyond AI.

> **TRY THIS**
>
> Take an AI response you received recently for research. Score it honestly: Did it actually answer your question with specific, verifiable information? Or did it produce the appearance of helpfulness without the substance? Notice how critical evaluation changes what you accept.

Chapter Summary

Key takeaways:

- AI flips the research ratio: spend twenty percent on data gathering and eighty percent on analysis and meaning-making
- Start with a strong foundation—frameworks, context, and clear objectives produce dramatically better research
- The quality of your prompt determines the quality of your output—invest in building the right prompt before diving in

- Verification isn't optional—build a systematic approach to checking what AI gives you
- AI does exactly what you say, not necessarily what you want—your expertise provides the context and meaning that transforms data into insight
- Build knowledge progressively using your own notes and structured systems
- Know when AI isn't enough—primary sources, current events, and specialized expertise remain essential

What's next: Chapter 9 explores how AI can assist with decision-making—helping you clarify options, analyze tradeoffs, and think through complex choices.

"AI can help you learn faster. It can't replace the judgment that comes from genuine understanding."

Chapter 9: AI for Decision-Making

I've started using AI as a way to pressure-test my decisions—everything from buying the right microphone for my home office Zoom setup to evaluating the vendor landscape for a cybersecurity platform that will protect ten thousand employees.

What surprised me wasn't that AI changed my decisions. It's that it almost never did.

Every time my team and I have used AI to stress-test a vendor selection—running through the alternatives, comparing feature sets, analyzing pricing models, checking for disruptors on the horizon—we've ended up going with our original choice. But we arrived at that choice with significantly more data, more perspective, and more confidence. For the home purchases, AI helped me cut through the noise to find the optimal, most cost-effective option faster than I would have on my own.

The pattern taught me something important about how AI actually helps with decisions. It doesn't make better choices for you. It makes you a better-informed chooser. It pressure-tests your reasoning so that when you commit, you've earned that confidence rather than hoped for it.

This chapter explores using AI to improve how you make decisions—

not by outsourcing judgment, but by enhancing the thinking that leads to better choices.

CHAPTER OVERVIEW

What you'll learn: - How to use AI to clarify decisions without delegating them - Techniques for exploring options and analyzing tradeoffs - Methods for stress-testing your thinking - When AI helps decision-making and when it doesn't

Why it matters: Better decisions come from better thinking. AI can improve your thinking process.

Reading time: About 15 minutes

The Decision Support Mindset

When facing a difficult decision, your first instinct is often: "What should I do?" It's tempting to ask AI directly and hope for a clear answer.

That rarely works well. AI doesn't know your full situation. It can't weigh what matters to you. It lacks the context of your values, relationships, and history that inform good choices. And for important decisions—the ones that keep you up at night—abdicating to AI means abdicating responsibility.

A better approach: use AI to improve your thinking, not replace it.

AI can help you: - Clarify what you're actually deciding - Articulate options you might not have considered - Identify assumptions you're making - Analyze tradeoffs systematically - Anticipate consequences and risks - Stress-test your reasoning

AI cannot: - Know what you truly value - Account for context only you understand - Take responsibility for outcomes - Replace judgment developed through experience - Make choices feel right

The goal isn't getting AI to make decisions. It's using AI to make yourself a better decision-maker.

> **KEY POINT**
>
> Use AI to think more clearly, not to think less. The decision remains yours.

Clarifying the Decision

Many decisions feel difficult because they're unclear. What exactly are you choosing between? What's really at stake? What would each option actually mean?

AI excels at helping you articulate what you're facing.

Start with the confusion:

"I'm trying to decide whether to take a new job offer. But I'm finding it hard to think clearly about it. Can you help me articulate what I'm actually weighing?"

This invitation allows AI to ask questions that help you clarify: - What draws you to the new opportunity? - What would you be giving up? - What uncertainties are making this hard? - What would make the decision obvious in either direction?

Frame the real question:

Sometimes what seems like one decision is actually several. "Should I accept this job?" might actually be: "Do I want to leave my current job?" + "Is this the right next step?" + "Is the timing right?" Separating these can make each easier to think about.

Identify what you already know:

"Help me separate what I know from what I'm uncertain about. What facts do I have, and where am I guessing?"

This sorting often reveals that some concerns are based on assumptions rather than evidence—and assumptions can be checked.

Generating Options

When facing a decision, we often see fewer options than actually exist. AI can help expand your view.

Beyond the obvious:

"I'm thinking about X or Y. What other options might I be missing? Are there alternatives I haven't considered?"

Sometimes the best choice isn't among your initial options. There might be a third path, a hybrid approach, or a way to defer the decision until you have more information.

Creative combinations:

"Could I do some version of both? What would a hybrid look like?"

The do-nothing option:

"What happens if I don't decide? What are the consequences of maintaining the status quo?"

Often "not deciding" is itself a decision with consequences worth examining.

Questioning the frame:

"Am I asking the right question? Is there a different way to think about what I'm trying to accomplish?"

Sometimes the decision as framed obscures a better question. "Which job should I take?" might become "What kind of work do I want to be doing?" which leads to different options entirely.

TRY THIS

Think of a decision you're currently facing. Ask AI: "I'm deciding between [option A] and [option B]. What options might I be missing? Are there alternatives I haven't considered?" Notice what emerges.

Analyzing Tradeoffs

Most real decisions involve tradeoffs—you can't have everything. AI can help you examine these systematically.

Explicit tradeoff analysis:

"For each option, what am I gaining and what am I giving up? Help me see the tradeoffs clearly."

Seeing gains and losses side by side often clarifies what's really being weighed.

Weighted importance:

"Which of these tradeoffs matters most? Help me think about which factors should carry the most weight in this decision."

Not all considerations are equal. A small gain in something important might outweigh a large gain in something trivial.

Short-term versus long-term:

"How do these options look in the short term versus the long term? Am I sacrificing future benefit for immediate gain, or vice versa?"

Time horizon matters enormously. The right choice for the next year might be wrong for the next decade. When I evaluate cybersecurity vendors, I'm always looking over the horizon: Will this vendor keep innovating? Are they at least a fast follower? If not, I'll end up with a capability gap—and then the replacement headache starts. The immediate cost comparison matters far less than the five-year trajectory.

Reversibility:

"Which aspects of this decision are reversible and which aren't? What doors close permanently with each choice?"

Irreversible decisions deserve more careful analysis than easily-changed ones.

Stress-Testing Your Thinking

We all have biases that cloud our judgment. I've caught myself cherry-picking data to support a decision I'd already made emotionally—more than once. AI can help you challenge your own reasoning in ways that are hard to do alone.

This is where I've found AI most consistently valuable for decisions. Not in making the choice, but in making sure I've earned the choice. When my team evaluates a security platform, we've usually formed an initial opinion after the demos and technical reviews. AI's role isn't to decide for us—it's to make sure we haven't missed something. What are the strongest arguments for the competitor we're not choosing? What risks are we underweighting? What assumptions are baked into our evaluation criteria?

The devil's advocate:

"I'm leaning toward [option]. Play devil's advocate—what are the strongest arguments against this choice?"

Actively seeking counterarguments improves decision quality, but it's psychologically hard to argue against yourself. AI can do this without ego investment. This is the same devil's advocate technique from Chapter 6, applied to decisions rather than communication.

Assumption surfacing:

"What assumptions am I making with this decision? Which of these might be wrong?"

Often our reasoning rests on assumptions we haven't examined. Making them explicit allows you to test them.

Failure scenarios:

"If I choose [option] and it goes badly, what are the most likely reasons? What could go wrong?"

Pre-mortem analysis—imagining failure and working backward—helps identify risks you might otherwise miss.

The opposite view:

"Someone who disagreed with my conclusion might argue what? What's the best case for the other side?"

Genuinely understanding the opposing view strengthens your decision whether or not it changes your mind.

> **KEY POINT**
>
> The goal of stress-testing isn't to create doubt—it's to earn confidence. A decision that survives rigorous challenge is a decision you can trust.

Considering Consequences

Decisions create ripples. AI can help you trace them.

Immediate effects:

"What happens right after I make this choice? What are the immediate consequences?"

Second-order effects:

"And then what? What follows from those initial consequences? What chain of events might this set in motion?"

Looking beyond immediate results often reveals important considerations.

Effects on others:

"How does this decision affect other people? Who benefits, who's harmed, who needs to be consulted?"

Decisions rarely happen in isolation. Considering stakeholders improves both the decision and its implementation.

What you'll learn from it:

"What will I know after making this choice that I don't know now? How will my understanding change?"

Some decisions are partly experiments—they generate information that improves future choices.

When AI Doesn't Help

Not every decision benefits from AI involvement. And some of the most important ones actively resist it.

Decisions that live in healthy tension. Cybersecurity—my profession—is a perfect example. We need to deploy solutions fast to serve our customers. But we can't let speed create vulnerabilities, risks, or compliance gaps. Navigating this tension is a deeply human activity. It's not a binary yes or no. It's an understanding of the person you're talking with—their priorities, their pressures, whether they support your objectives or not. It's an understanding of your relationship and track record. It involves business judgment about the right answer given both the risks to the business and the risks to security.

Most real-world problems have two competing perspectives that are equally valid. The people who find the best solutions are the ones who can synthesize both sides rather than choosing one. This is where humans excel and AI does not. AI can lay out both sides of an argument clearly, but it can't navigate the political dynamics, the interpersonal trust, the organizational history, and the strategic judgment required to find the right path through that tension.

Decisions that require instinct. Sometimes you need to trust your gut. Over-analysis can obscure intuition that's actually well-founded—pattern recognition from years of experience that you can't fully articulate.

Decisions where you already know. If you know what you want to do but are looking for permission or validation, AI can't give you that. The answer is already inside you.

Decisions that need human input. Some decisions require conversations with people who have context AI lacks—colleagues, family members, mentors. AI can help you prepare for those conversations but can't replace them.

Decisions with inadequate information. When you don't have enough data to decide, the answer might be to gather more information rather than analyze what you have.

Trivial decisions. Not everything deserves deep analysis. Sometimes you should just choose and move on. Save your analytical energy for what matters.

> **THINK ABOUT IT**
>
> Consider your recent decisions. Which ones benefited from careful analysis? Which ones were better handled quickly? What determines whether a decision deserves systematic thinking?

Personal Decisions

AI can assist with personal decisions too, though with important caveats.

I tested this in the most personal way I could think of. I recorded a few days of ordinary conversation with my wife—just our daily interactions, nothing dramatic—and then asked AI how I could be a better husband.

The answer wasn't wrong about anything. But it wasn't enlightening either. The suggestions were reasonable: be more present, listen more actively, show more appreciation. All true. All things I already knew, deep down.

The gap isn't knowledge. At the human level, it comes down to facing ourselves and being willing to change. AI can mirror back what we're doing and suggest what we could do differently, but it can't provide the motivation, the humility, or the daily commitment that actual growth requires. That comes from within, or it doesn't come at all.

Career choices: AI can help you articulate what you value in work, analyze options, and anticipate tradeoffs. But it can't know what will make you fulfilled.

Relationship decisions: AI can help you think through situations more clearly, but decisions about relationships require emotional intelligence and values that you supply.

Financial decisions: AI can help you understand options and tradeoffs, but isn't a replacement for financial advice from qualified professionals when stakes are high.

Life direction: AI can help you explore what matters to you and what options exist. But questions of meaning and purpose are ultimately yours to answer.

For personal decisions, AI works best as a thinking partner—helping you clarify your own values and preferences rather than imposing external ones.

Using AI at Different Decision Stages

Different stages of decision-making benefit from different AI interactions.

Early stage (exploration):

- Open-ended questions
- Option generation
- Information gathering
- Understanding the landscape

At this stage, you want AI to help you see the full picture, not narrow your view prematurely. When I'm evaluating a new category of security technology, I start here—asking AI to map the vendor landscape, explain the underlying technology, and identify what differentiates the serious contenders from the noise.

Middle stage (analysis):

- Tradeoff analysis
- Stress-testing
- Consequence mapping
- Criteria development

Now you're doing the hard work of evaluation. AI helps you think systematically through what you've discovered. This is where the pressure-testing happens—challenging your initial impressions with data, counterarguments, and alternative perspectives.

Late stage (validation):

- Final devil's advocacy
- Implementation planning
- Decision documentation
- Communicating to others

Before committing, one final challenge to make sure you haven't missed something critical. Then AI can help you plan execution and communicate your choice to others.

A Decision-Making Workflow

For significant decisions:

1. **Clarify the decision.** "Help me articulate what I'm actually deciding. What's the real question?"
2. **Generate options.** "What choices do I have? What might I be missing?"
3. **Identify criteria.** "What factors should influence this decision? What matters most?"
4. **Analyze each option.** "For each option, how does it perform against my criteria? What are the tradeoffs?"
5. **Stress-test your thinking.** "What are the strongest arguments against my current inclination? What assumptions am I making?"
6. **Consider consequences.** "What follows from each choice? How does this affect others?"
7. **Make and document.** Once you've decided, note why. This helps you learn from the decision whether it turns out well or poorly.

For quick decisions:

Not every decision needs this full treatment. For lower-stakes choices, a simple "Here's my situation. What am I not thinking about?" might be sufficient. That's how I use AI for home purchases—quick landscape scan, quick comparison, done. Save the full workflow for the decisions that actually matter.

Learning from Decisions

AI can help you improve your decision-making over time.

After the fact:

"Here's how a decision turned out. Help me think about what I could have anticipated and what was genuinely unpredictable."

Good outcomes don't always mean good decisions, and bad outcomes don't always mean bad ones. Understanding what you could reasonably have known helps you improve.

Pattern recognition:

"I notice I tend to [pattern]. What might be driving that? Is it serving me well?"

We all have decision-making tendencies. Some are helpful, some aren't. Identifying patterns allows you to consciously reinforce or counteract them.

Chapter Summary

Key takeaways:

- Use AI to improve your thinking process, not to make decisions for you
- AI is most valuable as a pressure-tester—challenging your reasoning and expanding your perspective
- Clarify what you're actually deciding before trying to decide
- Generate options you might not have considered
- Stress-test your reasoning by actively seeking counterarguments
- Recognize that the most important decisions—navigating competing perspectives, building trust, facing yourself—remain deeply human
- AI can tell you what's correct without being enlightening; real growth requires facing yourself

What's next: Chapter 10 explores using AI for personal productivity—managing tasks, time, and attention more effectively.

"AI can help you think better about decisions. The choosing still belongs to you."

Chapter 10: AI for Personal Productivity

I realized something was changing when I noticed I was no longer dreading the admin backlog. The expense reports, the meeting prep, the routine correspondence—tasks that once consumed entire evenings now got handled during coffee breaks. Nothing felt rushed; I wasn't working harder. AI had become integrated into my workflow in ways I no longer consciously noticed.

The productivity gains weren't dramatic in any single instance. An email drafted in two minutes instead of fifteen. Meeting notes synthesized instantly instead of compiled manually. A presentation outline generated in seconds that I could then refine. Individually, none of these felt revolutionary. But multiplied across dozens of daily tasks, they added up to something significant—time returned, mental energy preserved, attention freed for work that actually mattered.

For my personal projects, the effect was even more dramatic. Between my day job, my board commitments, and everything else competing for my time, I might have a few hours a week for the things that matter most to me. Without AI integration, those hours would evaporate into setup and context-switching. With the persistent context systems from Chapter 5, I can do in three hours what used to take a hundred. That's not an exaggeration—it's the difference between making real progress and perpetually spinning wheels.

This chapter is about sustainable AI integration—building habits and systems that make you genuinely more productive without becoming dependent or exhausted.

> **CHAPTER OVERVIEW**
>
> **What you'll learn:** - How to identify high-impact productivity opportunities for AI - Patterns for integrating AI into daily workflows - Task management and prioritization with AI support - Building sustainable habits rather than chasing optimization
>
> **Why it matters:** Real productivity isn't about doing more—it's about doing what matters with less friction.
>
> **Reading time:** About 15 minutes

The Productivity Reality

Let's be honest about productivity and AI.

AI won't make you productive if you're disorganized. It won't prioritize your work if you don't know what matters. It won't give you focus if you're constantly distracted. AI amplifies your productivity systems—it doesn't replace them.

What AI can do: - Reduce friction on routine tasks - Handle the mundane parts of meaningful work - Help you think through what matters - Free mental energy for high-value activities

What AI cannot do: - Give you discipline or motivation - Make you care about your work - Create time that doesn't exist - Fix fundamentally broken workflows

This chapter assumes you have basic productivity habits—you know roughly what needs doing, you have some system for tracking tasks, you can focus when necessary. AI enhances those foundations. It doesn't create them.

KEY POINT

AI makes good productivity systems better. It doesn't fix bad ones.

Finding High-Impact Opportunities

Not every task benefits equally from AI assistance. The key is identifying where AI creates the most value for your particular work.

When I look at where AI saves me the most time, it's not the tasks I expected. The biggest wins aren't the complex, impressive-sounding ones. They're the death-by-a-thousand-cuts tasks—the ones that individually take five or ten minutes but collectively consume hours. Before AI integration, I'd spend Sunday evenings catching up on the week's administrative backlog. Now that backlog barely exists.

High-impact AI opportunities:

Routine with variation. Tasks that follow predictable patterns but require adapting to specific circumstances. Emails, reports, documentation—similar structure, different content each time. This turned out to be my single biggest time saver—routine correspondence that follows patterns but requires enough variation that templates don't work.

Starting from blank. Any task where you face a blank page or empty document. AI can provide a starting point to react to rather than nothing. This book is an example. I didn't ask AI to write my chapters. But having a structured outline to react to—to argue with, rearrange, and fill with my own experience—was dramatically more productive than staring at a blank document.

Information synthesis. When you need to combine information from multiple sources into something coherent. Meeting prep, research summaries, project updates.

Tedious precision. Tasks that require care but not creativity. Formatting, checking, organizing, standardizing.

Thinking through complexity. When you need to reason through something complicated. AI can be a thinking partner. I used this extensively when preparing a corporate analysis for a board of directors—not having AI write the analysis, but thinking through the implications of what I was finding, pressure-testing my reasoning before committing it to the final document.

Lower-impact AI opportunities:

Deep creative work. When the creative struggle is the point, AI shortcuts may undermine the result.

Simple tasks. If something takes 30 seconds without AI, adding AI doesn't help.

High-stakes precision. Legal, financial, or technical work where errors matter—AI can assist, but verification takes time.

Interpersonal tasks. Relationship-building, difficult conversations, emotional intelligence—these remain fundamentally human.

> **TRY THIS**
>
> Make a list of the tasks that consumed your time this past week. For each one, estimate: How much time would AI save? How much would quality improve? Focus AI integration on the items with the highest combined score.

Daily Workflow Integration

The most sustainable productivity gains come from routine integration—AI that's part of how you work, not something you have to remember to use.

I didn't arrive at my current workflow through careful planning. It evolved. I started using AI for one thing—drafting emails—and noticed I had time left over. So I added another integration. Then another. Over a few months, AI became woven into the rhythm of my day in ways I stopped consciously noticing. It's like driving a car you've driven for years. You don't think about each action. You just drive.

Morning planning:

"Here's what I have on my calendar today and my task list. Help me think through how to approach the day. What should I tackle first? Where do I need to prepare?"

This doesn't mean AI runs your day. It means AI helps you start the day with clarity rather than reactive scrambling. I find this most valuable on days packed with meetings—when the planning question isn't "what should I do?" but "what do I need to be prepared for?"

Email processing:

Instead of treating each email as a fresh challenge, develop patterns:

- Routine responses: "Draft a reply confirming receipt and indicating I'll respond in detail by Friday"
- Complex responses: Share the email and ask, "Help me think through how to respond to this"
- Batch processing: "Here are five emails I need to respond to. Draft responses for each"

The batch processing approach changed email from an ongoing interruption to a discrete task. I process emails in blocks rather than responding one at a time throughout the day. The result isn't just faster email—it's the reclaimed attention between emails that used to fragment my focus.

Meeting preparation:

"I have a meeting about [topic] with [people]. Based on what I've shared about the context, what should I be prepared to discuss? What questions might come up?"

The richness of this preparation depends entirely on the context you've built—which is why the persistent context systems from Chapter 5 matter so much in practice. When my AI has access to relevant project history and previous meeting notes, meeting prep goes from generic to genuinely useful—surfacing things I'd forgotten and connections I hadn't made.

End-of-day capture:

"Here's what I worked on today. Help me summarize progress and identify what needs attention tomorrow."

This creates a record you can use for weekly reviews, status updates, and context when picking up projects later. It's also the foundation for the kind of persistent context system we discussed in Chapter 5—each day's capture becomes tomorrow's starting point.

Task Management Support

AI can help you manage tasks more effectively—not by managing them for you, but by helping you think about them better.

Breaking down large tasks:

"I need to [large task]. Help me break this into concrete next steps. What's the first thing I should actually do?"

Overwhelm almost always comes from vague tasks. "Finish the report" feels impossible—and paralyzing. "Draft the introduction" feels doable. I've found that asking AI to break down my own task list is one of the highest-return habits I've developed. When I was writing this book, for instance, "write the chapter on AI ethics" sat on my list for weeks untouched. The moment I asked AI to help me break that into specific steps—outline the key themes, gather relevant personal stories, draft the opening anecdote, work through each section—it went from paralyzing to manageable. Not because the task got smaller, but because it became concrete.

Prioritization thinking:

"Here's my task list for this week. Help me think through what's actually most important versus what's most urgent. What should I do first if I can only complete three things?"

Estimating time:

"How long do you think each of these tasks will realistically take? Am I being too optimistic about what I can accomplish today?"

We chronically underestimate how long things take. AI can provide a reality check.

Identifying dependencies:

"Which of these tasks depends on other things being completed first? What's blocking what?"

Sometimes you're stuck because you're trying to do things in the wrong order.

Managing Information

One of AI's strongest contributions to productivity is managing the information flowing at you.

Summarizing input:

Long documents, dense emails, verbose reports—AI can extract what matters:

"Summarize this document. What are the key points I need to know? What action items does it suggest for me?"

Creating briefings:

"I have a meeting about [project] tomorrow. Based on the documents I've shared, create a one-page briefing of the current status, key issues, and questions we need to resolve."

Tracking multiple threads:

"I'm working on projects A, B, and C. Here's what happened this week on each. Help me create a consolidated update I can share with my manager."

Processing meeting notes:

"Here are my notes from today's meeting. Organize them into decisions made, action items, and topics for follow-up. Who's responsible for what?"

The Administrative Layer

The administrative work of professional life—expenses, scheduling, correspondence, documentation—consumes disproportionate time and energy for its importance. AI can handle much of this burden.

Expense reports:

"Here are my receipts from the business trip. Help me categorize them and draft the expense report. Flag anything that might need additional documentation."

Travel planning:

"I need to travel to [destination] for meetings on [dates]. What logistics do I need to arrange? Draft an itinerary and help me identify what to book."

Routine correspondence:

"I need to send a thank-you note to [person] for [reason]. Draft something appropriate for our relationship level."

Documentation:

"I just completed [project/task]. Help me document what was done, decisions made, and lessons learned for future reference."

Invoice processing:

"Review this invoice against our contract terms. Does it match what we agreed? Flag any discrepancies."

KEY POINT

Administrative tasks often aren't hard—they're just numerous. AI handles the volume so you can focus on exceptions that need your judgment.

Learning and Development

AI can accelerate your learning and skill development in sustainable ways.

I experienced this firsthand when I decided to build a full application ecosystem—a personal AI assistant with voice capabilities, health integration, and enterprise-grade security. I don't know how to code in the traditional sense. I've never taken a programming course. But I needed to understand enough about encryption, database design, and how software components talk to each other to direct AI agents effectively. AI became my just-in-time tutor—explaining concepts at the level of depth I needed, exactly when I needed them, in the context of what I was actually building.

Just-in-time learning:

When you need to learn something for immediate application:

"I need to understand [concept] well enough to [apply it]. Give me the practical essentials."

This isn't deep expertise. It's functional knowledge when you need it. When I needed to understand post-quantum cryptography for my app's encryption layer, I didn't need a PhD-level explanation. I needed to understand enough to make good architectural decisions. AI gave me exactly that—no more, no less.

Skill building:

"I want to get better at [skill]. What are the key areas to focus on? How would you suggest I practice?"

AI can provide structure and feedback for deliberate practice.

Explaining what you encounter:

When you run into something unfamiliar:

"I just encountered [term/concept/approach]. Explain what this is and why it matters."

This turns confusion into learning moments.

Processing what you read:

"I just read [book/article]. Help me articulate the key insights and how they might apply to my work."

Active processing beats passive consumption.

Sustainable Habits

The goal isn't maximum AI usage. It's sustainable integration that makes you more effective over time.

Start small:

Don't try to AI-enable everything at once. Pick one recurring task and develop a reliable pattern. Once that's automatic, add another.

Friction matters:

If using AI feels like extra work, you won't do it. The integration should reduce friction, not add it. If accessing AI takes multiple steps, it won't become habitual.

Know when to skip:

Some days, the overhead of explaining context to AI isn't worth it. The task is small enough or you're in a flow state where AI would be interruption. That's fine. Sustainable use means using AI when it helps, not forcing it where it doesn't.

Regular review:

Periodically ask yourself: Is this AI integration actually helping? What's working? What's friction without benefit? Adjust accordingly.

Beware optimization obsession:

There's always a better prompt, a more efficient workflow, a smarter integration. At some point, the optimization effort costs more than it saves. Good enough is often good enough. I've caught myself spending thirty minutes refining a prompt template that saves me two minutes per use. That math only works if I use it fifteen times—and I usually don't. The discipline of recognizing when you're optimizing for optimization's sake, rather than for actual productivity, is itself a productivity skill.

Personal Systems

What works for productivity depends on how you work. Here are patterns to adapt, not prescriptions to follow.

The capture system:

Use AI to process raw captures into organized form:

"Here are my random notes from today. Help me turn these into actionable items, things to remember, and ideas to explore later."

The weekly review:

"Here's what I planned to do this week and what actually happened. Help me assess: What worked? What didn't? What should change next week?"

The project pulse:

For ongoing projects, periodic AI-assisted status checks:

"Based on where this project is, what should I be worried about? What's going well? What needs attention before next week?"

The communication audit:

"Here are the emails/messages I sent this week. Do you notice any patterns? Am I communicating effectively, or is something off?"

External perspective on your communication can reveal blind spots.

Building Your Personal Knowledge System

Beyond daily productivity, there's a more ambitious integration: building an AI-powered personal knowledge system that captures, organizes, and makes accessible your accumulated experience. In Chapter 5, we talked about how providing context transforms AI's usefulness. A personal knowledge system takes that principle to its logical conclusion—systematically capturing your context so it's always available.

The idea grew out of the persistent context files I was creating for software projects—capturing decisions, patterns, and accumulated learning that made AI dramatically more useful over time. But the same principle applied to everything else in my professional life. What if I could give AI access to not just my current project, but my entire professional history?

Consider what most professionals accumulate over years:

- **Conversations:** Meeting notes, emails, phone calls, messages
- **Published content:** LinkedIn posts, articles, presentations
- **Documents:** Reports, proposals, research
- **Reading:** Book notes, article highlights, annotations
- **Ideas:** Scattered notes, evolving thoughts, insights

This intellectual wealth typically remains scattered—useful in the moment, lost afterward. AI can change that.

The multi-source integration pattern:

The key insight is that AI can treat diverse information sources uniformly. Whether content comes from email, a messaging platform, or personal notes, the same processing applies:

1. **Capture:** Pull content from wherever it lives
2. **Normalize:** Structure it in consistent format
3. **Extract:** Identify key elements—people mentioned, ideas discussed, decisions made
4. **Index:** Make it searchable
5. **Connect:** Surface relationships between ideas across sources

What becomes possible:

Content mining: "Find every time I've discussed leadership development in the past year—in emails, meeting notes, and messages. What patterns emerge?"

Relationship intelligence: "When did I last interact with Sarah? What did we discuss? What commitments did I make?"

Idea genealogy: "How has my thinking about AI governance evolved? Show me the progression across my writing."

Voice analysis: "How does my communication style differ when writing to executives versus technical teams? What patterns should I maintain for consistency?"

How I built mine:

I built a personal knowledge system—a digital twin, essentially—that pulls from over twenty years of accumulated content: - Meeting transcripts (thousands of conversations captured through tools like Limitless and Otter) - LinkedIn posts and articles (years of professional writing) - Graduate school papers and professional documents - Email correspondence - Personal notes and evolving ideas

The system doesn't just store this content—it understands it. It extracts contacts automatically, tracking who was mentioned, interaction history, and relationship context. It identifies quotes and stories that might be useful for writing. It analyzes my voice patterns across different audiences. Daily automated syncs keep everything current.

The result is something I find genuinely powerful: a queryable version of my professional memory. When writing a board presentation, searching "board governance discussions" surfaces relevant ideas from months of conversations I'd otherwise have forgotten. When preparing for a meeting with someone I haven't seen in months, pulling their interaction history provides instant context—what we discussed, what I committed to, what matters to them.

This book is itself a product of that system. When I needed stories and examples for a chapter, I could search across everything I've said, written, and discussed over years. The system surfaced connections I wouldn't have remembered—conversations from months ago that perfectly illustrated a point I was trying to make. It's not replacing my memory; it's extending it.

Starting smaller:

You don't need to build an elaborate system. Start with one content stream:

1. **Weekly capture:** Each Friday, compile the week's significant communications, decisions, and ideas
2. **AI processing:** Ask AI to extract key themes, people mentioned, and commitments made
3. **Simple storage:** Keep processed summaries in organized files
4. **Monthly synthesis:** Ask AI to identify patterns across the month's captures

This basic rhythm—capture, process, synthesize—creates compounding value. After six months, you have a searchable record of your professional life. After a year, patterns become visible that weren't apparent in the moment.

TRY THIS

Pick one week's worth of emails. Ask AI: "Extract every person mentioned, commitment I made, and idea discussed. Organize by theme." See what emerges from structured processing of content you'd otherwise forget.

The configuration mindset:

As your system grows, treat configuration as the main work:

- Define what sources feed the system
- Establish how often each source syncs
- Create categories for organizing content
- Set triggers for automatic processing

The actual processing becomes automated. Your job is designing the system, not running it manually.

Voice across audiences:

One valuable output from a personal knowledge system is understanding your own communication patterns. AI can analyze how your writing differs across contexts:

Audience	Communication Style
Board/Executive	Concise, strategic, outcome-focused
Technical teams	Detailed, precise, example-rich
Peers	Collaborative, idea-sharing, balanced
Personal	Casual, warm, relationship-focused

Understanding these patterns helps maintain consistency and authenticity across contexts. When you need to write for a particular audience, you have examples of what works.

Privacy considerations:

A personal knowledge system raises legitimate privacy concerns—ones I take seriously enough that they shaped the entire architecture of my system. I built mine on a database that only I control, encrypted with post-quantum cryptography, specifically because I didn't want my professional memory living on someone else's servers.

- Who else has access to this data?
- Where is it stored?
- What happens to sensitive information?

If building such a system, think carefully about what you're comfortable capturing and where it lives. Keeping data on your own computer gives you control. Cloud-based systems—where your data lives on someone else's servers—offer convenience but require trusting those providers. The choice depends on your comfort level and the sensitivity of what you're processing. We'll explore the deeper ethical dimensions of this—including where your consciousness ends and the technology begins—in Chapter 14.

What Productivity Isn't

A word about what AI-enabled productivity shouldn't become.

Not overwork. If AI helps you do more work, the goal isn't to fill every freed minute with additional work. That path leads to burnout with better tools. Time returned should include time for rest, relationships, and activities that aren't optimizable.

Not perfection-seeking. AI makes it easy to revise endlessly. "Good enough" remains a valid standard. Don't let AI enable unhealthy perfectionism.

Not replacement for thinking. The efficiency gains shouldn't come from skipping thought. They should come from handling the parts that don't require thought so you can think better about what does.

Not measurement obsession. Tracking productivity can be useful. Obsessing over metrics is counterproductive. The goal is to do meaningful work well, not to maximize measurable output.

THINK ABOUT IT

What would you do with an extra hour per day? An extra five hours per week? Productivity gains only matter if you use the freed time well. What matters enough to warrant the investment?

Building Your System

There's no universal AI productivity system. The right approach depends on your work, your style, and your goals.

Questions to guide your system design:

- Where does your time currently go? What's disproportionate?
- What tasks drain you most? What do you avoid?
- Where do small improvements compound into big benefits?
- What fits naturally into how you already work?
- What's the minimum viable AI integration that helps?

Start with these high-impact areas:

1. **One routine communication** - Daily emails, regular reports, recurring correspondence
2. **One planning ritual** - Weekly planning, daily prioritization, project kickoffs
3. **One information synthesis task** - Meeting prep, document summaries, research synthesis

Get these working reliably before expanding.

The Compounding Effect

The real power of AI productivity isn't any single time saved. It's the compound effect.

Small daily efficiencies accumulate into hours per week. Hours per week become days per month. Days per month translate to meaningful changes in what you can accomplish—or meaningful reductions in how hard you have to work for the same output.

I can trace this compounding in my own experience. The first month, AI saved me perhaps five hours a week—mostly email and administrative tasks. But each efficiency created space for the next integration. The time I reclaimed from email went into building better context systems. Better context made every AI interaction more productive. More productive interactions freed more time. After six months, I wasn't just saving time on individual tasks—I'd fundamentally changed what was possible in the hours I had available. Four published books, an application ecosystem, and a personal knowledge base—all built alongside a full-time job and board commitments. Not because AI did the work for me, but because it removed enough friction that my available hours could go toward what actually mattered.

But this compounding only happens with consistent integration. Occasional AI use doesn't compound. Sustainable daily habits do.

The goal isn't dramatic transformation. It's steady improvement that accumulates without requiring constant attention.

Chapter Summary

Key takeaways:

- AI amplifies existing productivity systems—it doesn't replace them
- Focus AI integration on high-impact opportunities: routine tasks, blank pages, information synthesis
- Build sustainable habits rather than chasing maximum optimization
- The goal is meaningful work with less friction, not maximum output
- Small efficiencies compound into significant gains over time

What's next: Part 4 shifts to broader implications—how AI is changing work, organizations, and careers, and how to navigate these changes.

"Productivity isn't about doing more. It's about doing what matters with less friction. AI can help with the friction part."

Chapter 11: The Changing Workforce

Remember my security team from Chapter 1—the one handling 600,000 incidents a year with just six analysts? I want to return to that story, because it illustrates something bigger than cybersecurity.

Those six analysts aren't doing what analysts did five years ago. Automation and AI handle the volume—deterministic systems process routine cases, AI enriches data and accelerates triage. Only about 2,000 to 3,000 incidents actually require human attention—the complex cases, the judgment calls, the situations where experience and intuition matter.

This isn't a story about job elimination. It's a story about job transformation. My analysts spend their time on genuine threat hunting, strategic defense, and the complex analysis that machines can't do. Their work is more valuable, more interesting, and more impactful than before automation.

This chapter examines how AI is changing work—not with speculation, but with what's actually happening. The story is more nuanced than either the utopian or dystopian narratives suggest.

CHAPTER OVERVIEW

What you'll learn: - What's actually happening to jobs as AI advances - The difference between job elimination and job transformation - Which skills become more valuable in an AI-enabled workplace - How to prepare yourself for ongoing change

Why it matters: Understanding the real trends helps you position yourself for the future, not the fears.

Reading time: About 18 minutes

Beyond the Headlines

The headlines oscillate between extremes. "AI Will Replace Millions of Jobs" competes with "AI Creates More Jobs Than It Destroys." Both framings miss what's actually happening.

Here's the reality: Research consistently shows that AI transforms jobs more than it eliminates them. As of early 2026, the Yale Budget Lab's ongoing labor market analysis has found no correlation between a job's AI exposure and unemployment changes. Goldman Sachs research (Briggs & Kodnani, 2023) estimated that about 7% of US employment could face displacement from generative AI—but that most affected jobs would be complemented rather than replaced, and that AI could boost global GDP by 7% over a decade.

More importantly, these numbers miss the transformation story. Jobs aren't simply appearing or disappearing. They're changing. The work within roles shifts. New capabilities enable new activities. Old tasks become automated while new tasks emerge.

Think about what happened to accountants when spreadsheet software arrived. Did accountants disappear? No. But what accountants do changed dramatically. The manual calculation work went away. Analysis, interpretation, and advisory work expanded. The profession transformed rather than vanished.

AI represents a similar transition—broader in scope, faster in pace, but following the same pattern of transformation rather than simple replacement.

KEY POINT

The question isn't "Will AI take my job?" It's "How will AI change my job—and am I ready?"

What's Actually Happening

Based on real workplace data and research, here's how AI is affecting different types of work:

Tasks automated, jobs transformed:

Most knowledge work involves a mix of routine and non-routine tasks. AI automates the routine parts, which changes the composition of the job rather than eliminating it.

- Legal research becomes faster, so lawyers spend more time on strategy and client counsel
- Financial analysis gets automated, so analysts focus more on interpretation and recommendation
- Customer service handles routine queries automatically, so representatives handle complex and sensitive cases
- Medical diagnosis gets AI-assisted, so doctors spend more time on patient communication and treatment planning

The pattern is consistent: AI handles the routine, humans handle the exceptions and the judgment.

New capabilities, expanded scope:

AI doesn't just take away tasks—it enables new ones. My security team can now do threat hunting that wasn't possible when all their time went to routine triage. Writers can explore more drafts. Researchers can cover more ground. Managers can make more data-informed decisions.

When the cost of certain activities drops dramatically, people do more of those activities. That's not job loss—it's job evolution.

Entirely new roles:

Some jobs that barely existed a few years ago are now in demand: AI trainers, prompt engineers, AI ethics specialists, human-AI workflow designers. Technology transitions consistently create roles that weren't anticipated.

Jobs at genuine risk:

Some roles are at significant risk. Jobs that consist almost entirely of routine cognitive tasks that AI handles well—certain data entry, basic analysis, routine writing—face real pressure. But even here, the story is usually reduction and transformation rather than elimination.

The Skills Shift

As AI handles more routine cognitive work, the labor market is repricing certain human skills. This isn't speculation—it's showing up in hiring data, compensation trends, and organizational restructuring.

Critical thinking is in demand and short supply.

In a Hart Research Associates survey (2018), 78% of business executives ranked critical thinking as the most important skill they want in employees—yet only 34% of college graduates arrive prepared with it. That gap has only widened. When AI can generate plausible-sounding content on any topic, organizations need people who can evaluate, question, and judge what AI produces.

Ambiguity tolerance commands a premium.

Problems with clear solutions become easier to automate. The problems that remain—navigating competing stakeholder interests, making calls with incomplete information, weighing tradeoffs that involve values—these are what organizations struggle to fill.

Interpersonal skills are the new technical skills.

Persuasion, negotiation, coalition-building, and leading diverse teams—these were always valuable, but now they're becoming the core of many roles as routine cognitive work shifts to AI.

Learning velocity matters more than credentials.

Learning itself may be more valuable than any specific thing learned. Organizations increasingly hire for adaptability alongside domain expertise. Technical skills have shorter half-lives; the ability to acquire new capabilities quickly is the meta-skill underlying everything else.

The AI-fluent domain expert is the new unicorn.

The most sought-after combination in the workforce is deep domain knowledge paired with the ability to work effectively with AI. Either alone is less valuable than both together. (We'll explore how to build this combination for your own career in Chapter 13.)

> **THINK ABOUT IT**
>
> Consider your current role. What percentage of your time goes to tasks AI could potentially handle? What percentage goes to judgment, relationships, and complex problem-solving? How has this ratio changed over the past few years?

The Transformation Story

Here's how transformation looks in practice.

When I took over security operations, we had a traditional model: analysts triaged alerts, most of which were noise. It was frustrating work. Good analysts burned out. The backlog never ended.

We implemented automation progressively. First, deterministic systems handled the clearly-false-positive patterns. Then ML models learned to categorize alerts. Then AI enrichment added context to help with triage decisions.

Each step reduced the routine workload. But we didn't eliminate analysts. We changed what they do. Instead of clicking through thousands of routine alerts, they now investigate genuine threats. Instead of repetitive triage, they do threat hunting—proactively looking for signs of compromise that automated systems miss.

The job became more interesting and more valuable. Junior analysts accelerate to senior capabilities faster because they're not spending years on mindless triage. The team's strategic impact increased dramatically.

This transformation required the analysts to change too. They needed to learn to work with automated systems, understand what the AI was doing, know when to trust it and when to override it. Those who couldn't adapt struggled. Those who could thrived.

That's the story playing out across industries: not replacement, but transformation that rewards adaptation.

Who Thrives, Who Struggles

In my experience leading teams through transformation, outcomes vary dramatically—and not always for the reasons you'd expect. I see this playing out in real time across two very different worlds I operate in.

I work with several startup founders who are aggressively adopting AI—building with 80 to 90 percent of their development driven by AI tools. They're leapfrogging competitors who are still coding everything by hand. These are small teams with clean slates: no legacy systems, no regulatory baggage, no decades of established processes to protect. When a new AI capability emerges, they integrate it within days. Their speed of iteration is staggering. They're building products that would have required ten-person engineering teams three years ago, and they're doing it with two or three people and AI.

Meanwhile, in my day job in healthcare—specifically health insurance—the picture couldn't be more different. Healthcare is heavily regulated. HIPAA governs how every piece of patient data can be used, stored, and processed. There's almost no room for error. The workforce has deep expertise built over decades in pre-AI processes. You can't simply hand an AI tool to a claims processor or care manager and say "go faster." You need thoughtful change management, retraining, privacy safeguards, and careful validation that AI isn't introducing errors into decisions that affect people's health coverage.

Neither approach is wrong. The startups thrive because their context allows aggressive adoption. Healthcare organizations adapt more carefully because their context *demands* it—lives and livelihoods depend on getting it right. The mistake would be for either to imitate the other. The startup that moves cautiously like a hospital loses its competitive edge. The hospital that moves recklessly like a startup puts patients at risk.

Here's what separates those who thrive from those who struggle—at both the individual and organizational level:

Those who thrive:

- Embrace AI as a capability rather than viewing it as threat
- Continuously learn and adapt
- Focus on developing skills that complement AI rather than compete with it
- Take ownership of their professional development
- Look for opportunities to create value in new ways
- Match their adoption pace to their context—fast when the situation allows, careful when it demands

Those who struggle:

- Resist change and hope the transformation doesn't reach them
- Stop learning when formal education ends
- Try to protect routine work rather than moving to higher-value activities
- Wait for their organization to tell them what to do
- Define their value by tasks rather than outcomes
- Either move too fast for their context or too slow for their opportunity

The difference isn't intelligence or even initial skill level. It's mindset, behavior, and contextual awareness.

KEY POINT

The formula from Chapter 1 still holds: critical thinking, continuous upskilling, and ownership of your development. But now you can see why it works—these are precisely the capabilities AI cannot replicate. The question is whether you're driving the change or being driven by it.

Preparing for Ongoing Change

The AI transformation isn't a one-time event to survive. It's an ongoing evolution to navigate. Here's how to prepare:

Stay current without panicking:

Pay attention to how AI is affecting your field. Follow developments without catastrophizing. Understand what's changing and why. Make decisions based on trends, not headlines.

Invest in durable skills:

Some skills remain valuable across technology transitions: critical thinking, communication, leadership, ethical reasoning, creativity. These take time to develop. Start now.

Build AI fluency:

You don't need to become a technical expert, but you do need to work effectively with AI tools. This book is part of that investment. Keep practicing, keep learning, keep expanding what you can do.

Experiment proactively:

Don't wait for your organization to tell you how to use AI. Experiment on your own. Find ways to improve your work. Become the person who understands how AI applies to your domain.

Network and stay visible:

In periods of change, opportunities often come through relationships. Stay connected to your professional community. Share what you're learning. Be known as someone who's adapting successfully.

Develop a learning practice:

How fast you learn matters more than what you currently know. Build a personal system for acquiring new capabilities—whether that's dedicated learning time, structured experimentation, or deliberate practice. Make it a habit, not an occasional event.

Organizational Implications

While this chapter focuses on individual preparation, organizations also face transformation challenges.

The talent equation shifts:

Organizations can often accomplish more with fewer people when AI handles routine work. But they need different people—those who can work with AI effectively, exercise judgment on complex cases, and adapt continuously.

Hiring changes:

Some organizations are already hiring differently. They look for adaptability and learning capacity alongside domain expertise. Technical skills have shorter half-lives; meta-skills matter more.

Reskilling becomes essential:

Organizations that help their people transform tend to fare better than those that simply replace workers. Institutional knowledge and cultural fit have value that's lost in layoffs and rehiring. This is a leadership challenge as much as a technology challenge—something I've seen repeatedly in cybersecurity transformation initiatives. Leaders who invest in their people's development create cultures that adapt; leaders who treat workers as replaceable costs create cultures that stagnate.

New structures emerge:

The traditional hierarchy may not fit AI-augmented work. When AI handles much of the routine coordination, what does management look like? Organizations are experimenting with new structures.

Industry Variations

AI impacts different industries differently. Some patterns:

Knowledge work transformation:

Law, finance, consulting, medicine, education—knowledge work across sectors is transforming. Routine analysis and research become AI-assisted. Human focus shifts to judgment, relationships, and complex problem-solving.

Creative industries:

Writing, design, media, entertainment—creative fields see AI as both tool and threat. The pattern so far: AI augments creative work more than it replaces it, but changes what "creative work" means.

Manufacturing and operations:

Physical work transforms differently than knowledge work. Robotics and AI together change manufacturing, logistics, and operations—but physical constraints limit the pace of change compared to purely digital work.

Service industries:

Customer service, healthcare delivery, education—services that involve human relationships see AI handling routine interactions while humans handle complex and emotionally sensitive ones.

Tech itself:

The technology industry is transforming rapidly. AI changes how software is built, how systems are operated, how products are developed. The people building AI tools are themselves being augmented by AI.

Honest Uncertainties

It would be dishonest to pretend we know exactly how this unfolds. Some genuine uncertainties:

Pace of change:

AI capabilities are advancing faster than many expected. Whether this pace continues, accelerates, or plateaus affects everything.

Economic distribution:

Will AI-enabled productivity gains be broadly shared, or will benefits concentrate among those who own and control AI systems? This is as much a political question as a technical one.

Transition smoothness:

Will changes be gradual enough for adaptation, or will some sectors face rapid disruption that overwhelms adjustment capacity?

New possibilities:

AI might enable entirely new industries and opportunities we can't currently imagine. Technology transitions often create more than they destroy, but the new things take time to emerge.

Human responses:

How people, organizations, and societies respond to AI will shape outcomes as much as the technology itself. We have agency here.

Given these uncertainties, the wisest approach is building adaptability—positioning yourself to do well across many scenarios rather than betting on one prediction.

The Dreamer Premium

Here's something I've observed: the dreamers will always have jobs.

AI isn't replacing vision and big-picture thinking. It's not generating genuine strategic insight. It's not imagining possibilities that don't exist yet. These remain distinctly human capabilities.

In a world where AI can execute many routine tasks, the ability to know what tasks are worth doing becomes more valuable. Strategy, vision, creativity, and meaning-making—these form a "dreamer premium" that AI enhances rather than replaces.

If you can articulate what should be created, AI helps you create it faster. If you can see opportunities others miss, AI helps you pursue them. If you can imagine better futures, AI helps you build toward them.

The key is developing that capacity for vision and meaning—and combining it with the practical ability to work with AI to realize it.

> **TRY THIS**
>
> Write down three ways your role might change over the next five years due to AI. For each, identify: What new skills would you need? What current activities might decrease? What might you be able to accomplish that's currently impossible? Use this as input for your professional development planning.

Chapter Summary

Key takeaways:

- AI transforms jobs more than it eliminates them—the pattern is change, not disappearance
- Skills like critical thinking, complex problem-solving, and communication become more valuable
- Those who thrive embrace AI as capability and invest in continuous learning
- Preparation requires building durable skills, AI fluency, and adaptability
- The "dreamer premium"—vision, meaning, creativity—remains distinctly human

A question to sit with:

If your job transformed tomorrow, what would you grieve? What would you celebrate? The answer tells you something important about what you actually value in your work—and what's worth protecting as AI changes everything around it.

What's next: Chapter 12 examines how organizations are approaching AI—strategies, governance, and what makes some organizations succeed while others struggle.

"This isn't job elimination; it's job transformation. The question is whether you're driving the change or being driven by it."

Chapter 12: How Organizations Should Approach AI

A fellow CISO pulled me aside after an industry event. "We have a problem," she said. "78% of our employees are using AI tools we didn't approve. They're putting company data into systems we don't control. They're making decisions based on AI outputs we can't verify. And I only found out because someone accidentally pasted confidential information into a public AI chat."

I wasn't surprised. I'd been dealing with the same thing in my own organization. This is the "Shadow AI" problem—employees using unapproved AI tools with company data—and it's happening everywhere. Employees aren't waiting for official guidance. They're using AI to make their work easier right now, regardless of policies or approvals. The genie is out of the bottle.

But the solution isn't to lock down AI access. That just drives it further underground. The organizations that succeed with AI find a different path: enabling AI use responsibly rather than either ignoring it or prohibiting it.

This chapter explores how organizations should approach AI—the strategy, governance, and cultural changes that separate successful adoption from chaos.

CHAPTER OVERVIEW

What you'll learn: - Why AI adoption is a cultural change, not just a technology deployment - The principles of effective AI governance - How to enable AI use while managing risks - What separates organizations that thrive from those that struggle

Why it matters: How your organization approaches AI affects your ability to use it effectively.

Reading time: About 18 minutes

The Strategic Question

Before diving into governance and policies, organizations need to answer a strategic question: What role will AI play in our future?

This isn't a yes-or-no question. Organizations sit somewhere on a spectrum:

AI as occasional tool. Employees use AI when helpful, but it's not central to operations. Think of it like office software—useful, but not transformative.

AI as capability multiplier. AI systematically augments what the organization can do. Processes are redesigned around AI capabilities. People's roles evolve to work with AI.

AI as competitive differentiator. AI becomes core to how the organization creates value. Products, services, and operations are fundamentally AI-enabled.

Where your organization should be depends on your industry, competitive position, and strategic goals. But making this explicit matters because the approach to governance, investment, and culture follows from the strategic intent.

Most organizations underestimate the scope of change required. They treat AI like previous technology deployments—install the software, train the users, move on. But AI touches how people think and work in ways that spreadsheets and email never did.

I learned this directly when I led a pilot program deploying AI coding tools to about fifty developers across six teams. We started thinking it was a technology deployment—get the licenses, configure the tools, let people code. Within the first week, it was clear we'd underestimated the scope of what we were actually changing. The tool wasn't just writing code faster. It was changing how developers thought about their work, how teams communicated, how quality was assessed, and how security operated. The organizations that succeed treat AI adoption as organizational transformation, not technology implementation.

> **KEY POINT**
>
> AI adoption is a cultural and organizational change, not just a technology deployment. Treating it as merely technical guarantees struggle.

The Governance Imperative

Effective AI governance enables responsible use at scale. Without it, you get Shadow AI: uncontrolled use that creates risk without organizational benefit.

Core governance principles:

Discover and document. You can't govern what you can't see. Organizations need visibility into what AI systems are being used, where, and for what purposes. This isn't surveillance—it's situational awareness.

Risk-based approach. Not all AI use carries equal risk. Using AI to draft internal emails differs from using AI to make customer-facing decisions. Governance should match the level of oversight to the level of risk.

Enable, don't just restrict. If governance only says "no," people work around it. Effective governance says "here's how to do this safely" rather than just prohibiting.

Clear accountability. When AI contributes to a decision or output, who's responsible? Governance should establish clear accountability rather than creating ambiguity.

Continuous evolution. AI capabilities and best practices change rapidly. Governance frameworks need built-in mechanisms for adaptation.

A Practical Governance Framework

Here's a framework that balances enablement with risk management:

Tier 1: Approved for general use.

AI tools and applications approved for routine use without additional oversight. Clear guidelines for appropriate use cases. Examples: approved AI assistants for drafting, research, and ideation.

Tier 2: Approved with controls.

AI use cases that require specific safeguards. Might include human review requirements, data handling restrictions, or documentation requirements. Examples: AI-assisted customer communication, AI in hiring processes.

Tier 3: Requires approval.

AI applications that need specific evaluation before deployment. High-risk use cases, sensitive data involvement, or novel applications. Involves legal, security, and ethics review as appropriate.

In our developer pilot, we lived this framework in practice. Basic code suggestions fell into Tier 1—developers could accept or reject them freely. But AI-generated code that pulled external packages or shelled out system commands was Tier 2—it required code review and automated security scanning before deployment. And any proposal to give AI access to production systems or customer data required Tier 3 evaluation. The framework wasn't just organizational neatness. It was the difference between enabling productivity and introducing uncontrolled risk.

The triage question.

For each AI system or use case, ask: "Is it necessary?" This simple question surfaces whether the benefit justifies the governance burden. Not everything that can use AI should use AI.

> **TRY THIS**
>
> Think about AI use in your organization. Which applications would fall into each tier? What use cases are currently happening without clear governance? Where is the gap between actual use and approved use largest?

Security and Risk Management

AI introduces specific security and risk considerations that organizations must address.

Data exposure risks:

When employees paste company information into AI tools, that data potentially leaves organizational control. Some considerations:

- What data should never go into external AI systems?
- What contractual protections exist with AI vendors?
- How do you verify that sensitive data isn't being inadvertently shared?

In my security work, I've found that roughly one out of every five log reviews turns up a credential or API key that someone accidentally exposed. AI interactions generate their own logs and records—and those records might contain sensitive information people didn't intend to share.

Output reliability risks:

AI can be confidently wrong. Organizations need to consider:

- What decisions rely on AI-generated information?
- What verification processes ensure accuracy?
- Who's accountable when AI outputs prove incorrect?

Security of AI systems:

As AI becomes embedded in operations, it becomes an attack vector. Considerations include:

- How could AI systems be manipulated or compromised?
- What happens if an AI system misbehaves?
- How do you detect AI systems behaving unexpectedly?

I tell my security teams: AI systems are already finding ways around guardrails. They discover unexpected paths around controls, and security teams need to anticipate this. In our pilot, we embedded industry security standards—OWASP, NIST, and HIPAA—directly into the AI's configuration files, essentially teaching the tool our security rules before it wrote a single line of code. We wired IDE plugins so that every successful build automatically triggered a static security scan. But even with those guardrails, we still found issues. The key lesson: security-by-design helps, but it doesn't eliminate the need for human oversight. You need both the guardrails and the people watching what the guardrails miss.

The Legal and Regulatory Landscape

AI governance doesn't happen in a vacuum. Hundreds of governments worldwide have introduced or are considering AI-related laws. Organizations need to navigate this evolving landscape.

Key regulatory themes:

Transparency. Increasing requirements to disclose when AI is involved in decisions, especially decisions affecting people (hiring, credit, healthcare).

Risk management. Requirements for assessing and mitigating risks from AI systems, particularly high-risk applications.

Accountability. Clarity about who's responsible when AI systems cause harm.

Data rights. How AI intersects with privacy regulations like GDPR, CCPA, and their successors.

Practical approach:

High-maturity organizations engage legal and compliance early in AI initiatives—at the ideation stage, not after deployment. They build compliance into design rather than retrofitting it.

Triage is a key skill here—find your highest-risk systems and maintain an effective threshold for evaluating new ones. You can't give equal attention to every AI application. Focus governance energy where risk is highest.

Enabling AI Across the Organization

Governance creates the framework. But organizations also need to actively enable AI adoption to realize benefits.

Building AI fluency:

Most employees need help developing AI skills. This isn't just training on specific tools—it's developing the judgment to know when and how to use AI effectively.

Our pilot revealed something I didn't expect: the single biggest predictor of success wasn't technical skill—it was the quality of the requirements and context people provided to the AI. Developers who spent time specifying what they wanted upfront got dramatically better results than those who jumped straight to "write me some code." The best sessions started with detailed context about the existing system, the coding standards, and the specific problem—essentially the practices we explored in Chapter 5 applied to an organizational setting. This insight reshaped how we thought about training. It wasn't about teaching people to use a tool. It was about teaching them to think clearly about what they needed.

Providing approved tools:

If you want people to use AI responsibly, give them good approved options. When official tools are inadequate, people find unofficial alternatives. Invest in tools that actually help people do their work. During our pilot, we found that developers who received good tools with clear guidelines used them enthusiastically. The Shadow AI problem wasn't about rebellious employees—it was about the gap between what people needed and what the organization officially offered.

Creating space for experimentation:

Innovation requires room to try things. Organizations benefit from sanctioned spaces for AI experimentation—places where people can explore without full production governance requirements, while still maintaining basic guardrails. Our pilot functioned as exactly this kind of space—bounded enough to manage risk, open enough for genuine discovery.

Sharing learning:

Early adopters learn lessons that can benefit others. Create mechanisms for sharing what works, what doesn't, and what to watch out for. Teams that plugged natural-language grooming discussions into AI and had it auto-generate features and user stories were sharing that approach with other teams within weeks. The pilot became a learning engine, not just a technology test.

Change Management Reality

AI adoption is change management. The technology is actually the easy part. The hard part is helping people and processes adapt.

I watched this play out in real time during the developer pilot. Getting the tools configured and deployed took a few days. Getting fifty people to fundamentally change how they approached their work took months—and even then, the adoption was uneven in ways that taught me more than the technology itself did.

Addressing fear:

Many people fear AI will make their jobs obsolete. That fear is often exaggerated but not baseless. Organizations need honest communication:

- Be truthful about how work will change
- Invest in helping people adapt
- Create paths to new roles and skills
- Acknowledge uncertainty without creating panic

During our pilot, some developers initially saw AI coding tools as a threat—a sign that their skills were becoming obsolete. The ones who thrived were the ones who realized the opposite: AI made their expertise more valuable, not less. The AI could write boilerplate code quickly, but it took experienced developers to know whether the code was right, secure, and aligned with the system's architecture. Senior developers who embraced AI became dramatically more productive. Those who resisted found themselves working harder to produce what their AI-augmented colleagues produced more easily.

Managing resistance:

Some resistance to AI is legitimate concern about real risks. Some is change aversion. Distinguishing between them matters. Valid concerns deserve engagement; pure resistance requires different approaches. In our pilot, some of the best security improvements came from developers who were initially skeptical—they pushed us to think more carefully about guardrails, which made the whole program stronger.

Supporting early adopters:

People who embrace AI early often face friction from colleagues and systems not designed for AI-augmented work. Supporting early adopters helps them succeed and creates models for others to follow. Our most effective early adopters were the teams that wove AI into existing workflows—design, grooming, testing—rather than treating it as a separate activity. They demonstrated five-times-faster delivery on new projects, building proof-of-concept applications in hours that would have taken days.

Maintaining human connection:

As AI handles more routine work, organizations need to consciously maintain human connections. AI shouldn't become an excuse to depersonalize the workplace.

> **KEY POINT**
>
> Culture determines AI success more than technology. Organizations that build cultures of learning, adaptation, and responsible experimentation outperform those that don't.

What Separates Success from Failure

Having led the developer pilot, run AI governance discussions, and watched peers navigate AI adoption across industries, I've seen clear patterns distinguish success from failure. The pilot crystallized these patterns for me because I could watch them play out in real time across six different teams approaching the same tools with different cultures and leadership styles:

Successful organizations:

- Treat AI adoption as organizational transformation, not technology deployment
- Create clear governance that enables rather than just restricts
- Invest in building AI fluency across the workforce
- Start with pilot programs and expand based on learning
- Position security and compliance as enablers, not blockers
- Maintain clear human accountability for AI-assisted decisions
- Adapt continuously as capabilities and best practices evolve

Struggling organizations:

- Treat AI as just another technology to deploy
- Either ignore AI entirely or try to prohibit it
- Underinvest in training and capability building
- Attempt big-bang deployments without learning first
- Create governance that blocks everything or permits everything
- Lose track of where AI is actually being used
- Treat AI governance as a one-time project rather than ongoing function

The Culture Factor

If culture eats strategy for breakfast, it devours technology deployments by lunch. The cultural elements that matter most:

Psychological safety:

People need to feel safe admitting when AI-assisted work goes wrong. If mistakes are punished, people hide them—and learning stops. Cultures that treat errors as learning opportunities adapt faster.

Learning orientation:

Organizations that value continuous learning adapt to AI better than those expecting stable competencies. When "what you know" has a shorter shelf life, "how fast you learn" becomes the key variable.

Responsible experimentation:

The sweet spot is encouraging experimentation while maintaining appropriate guardrails. Too much caution misses opportunities. Too little creates unacceptable risks. Organizations need cultures that can hold both.

Human-AI collaboration mindset:

Organizations that frame AI as "replacing humans" struggle. Organizations that frame AI as "augmenting humans" fare better. The framing affects how people engage with AI tools and how AI initiatives are designed. The autonomy spectrum from Chapter 2 applies here too—organizations need to choose what level of AI autonomy fits each function, and those choices should evolve as trust and capability develop.

A Maturity Model

Organizations typically progress through stages of AI maturity:

Stage 1: Ad hoc.

AI use happens informally, individual by individual. No coordinated approach. Shadow AI is common. Governance is absent or ignored.

Stage 2: Emerging.

Organization recognizes AI's importance. Initial policies appear. Some approved tools exist. Training begins. Governance is reactive.

Stage 3: Defined.

Clear governance framework. Risk-based approach to different use cases. Systematic training programs. Designated accountability. Regular assessment of AI landscape.

Stage 4: Managed.

AI integrated into business processes. Metrics track AI impact and risks. Governance evolves with changing capabilities. Continuous improvement culture around AI use.

Stage 5: Optimizing.

AI is strategic capability. Organization actively shapes how AI develops within its context. Leading practices that others follow. Contributes to industry standards and best practices.

Most organizations today are between stages 1 and 3. Movement requires intentional effort, investment, and leadership commitment.

What Leaders Should Do

If you have organizational influence, here's where to focus:

Get visibility.

Understand what AI use is actually happening in your organization. You can't govern what you don't see.

Create governance.

Establish frameworks that enable responsible use. Start with the highest-risk use cases and expand from there.

Invest in capability.

Build AI fluency across the organization. This isn't a one-time training—it's ongoing development.

Model the behavior.

Leaders who use AI well give others permission to do the same. Leaders who ignore AI signal it doesn't matter. I made a point during our pilot of using the same tools myself—not just overseeing their deployment but building with them. When I demonstrated an entire application built in days using the same AI coding tools we were piloting, it changed the conversation from "should we adopt this?" to "how do we make this work at scale?"

Stay current.

AI capabilities and best practices evolve rapidly. What worked last year may not work next year. Build continuous learning into leadership practice.

THINK ABOUT IT

Where is your organization on the maturity model? What would move it to the next level? What's the biggest gap between your current state and where you need to be?

The Individual's Role

Even if you don't lead your organization's AI strategy, you have influence.

Be the example. Use AI responsibly and effectively. Show what good looks like.

Speak up. If you see governance gaps or risks, raise them constructively. If official tools are inadequate, advocate for better ones.

Help colleagues. Share what you learn. Help others build AI fluency.

Engage with governance. Participate in shaping policies rather than just complaining about them.

Take ownership. Don't wait for the organization to tell you exactly how to use AI. Experiment responsibly within appropriate boundaries.

Chapter Summary

Key takeaways:

- AI adoption is organizational transformation, not just technology deployment
- Effective governance enables responsible use rather than just restricting

- Security and compliance should position themselves as enablers of AI, not blockers
- Culture—learning orientation, psychological safety, responsible experimentation—determines outcomes
- Organizations progress through maturity stages; moving forward requires intentional effort

What's next: Chapter 13 brings Part 4 to a close with a focus on your individual career—how to position yourself for success in an AI-enabled world.

"Position security as an enabler of AI, not a blocker. Governance should help people use AI well, not prevent them from using it at all."

Chapter 13: AI and Your Career

I opened this book with a story about building an application in a single day—despite not having coded since the 1980s. AI assistants handled the programming. I handled the vision, the decisions, and the judgment about what the application needed to do.

That experience taught me something about careers in an AI world that I want to unpack now. The professional developers I know are now ten times more productive than before. They're building things that would have been impossible with manual coding alone. AI didn't make their skills obsolete—it amplified them. And someone like me, with domain expertise but no coding ability, could suddenly create things that were previously out of reach.

The lesson: the combination of domain knowledge and AI capability is more valuable than either alone. I understood what I wanted to build. AI helped me build it. Neither part could have succeeded without the other.

This chapter is about your career—how to think about professional development, which skills to cultivate, and how to position yourself for success in a world where AI capabilities keep expanding.

CHAPTER OVERVIEW

What you'll learn: - How to think about career development in an AI-influenced world - Which skills become more valuable as AI capabilities grow - Practical strategies for staying relevant across change - How to take agency in your own career path

Why it matters: The choices you make now about learning and development shape your professional future.

Reading time: About 15 minutes

The Career Question

"Will AI take my job?" is the wrong question. Here's the right one: "How is AI changing what's valuable in my work?"

The answer varies by field, but a pattern emerges consistently: AI handles the routine, leaving humans to focus on judgment, relationships, creativity, and novel problem-solving. Understanding this pattern helps you identify where to invest your development.

What AI does well:

- Pattern matching at scale
- Processing large volumes of information
- Generating content that follows established patterns
- Executing well-defined procedures
- Answering questions that have clear answers

What humans do better:

- Judgment in ambiguous situations
- Building relationships and trust
- Genuine creativity and innovation
- Understanding context and nuance
- Making meaning and setting direction
- Ethical reasoning and values-based decisions

Your career strategy should emphasize developing capabilities that complement AI rather than compete with it. The goal isn't to outperform AI at what AI does well—it's to excel at what AI can't do.

KEY POINT

Don't compete with AI on AI's strengths. Compete on distinctly human capabilities that AI amplifies rather than replaces.

The Skills Portfolio

When I look back at my own career path—from government consulting to cybersecurity leadership to writing books and building applications with AI—the skills that carried me weren't the technical ones. Technical knowledge mattered, but it was always evolving; what I knew about security in 2010 was largely obsolete by 2020. What endured were the skills AI still can't replicate: the judgment to know which risks actually matter, the ability to communicate complex ideas to non-technical leaders, and the willingness to keep learning when the ground shifts underneath you.

Think of your professional capabilities as a portfolio that needs active management. Some skills appreciate in value as AI advances; others depreciate.

Appreciating skills:

Critical thinking. Chapter 11 showed the workforce demand. Here's the career implication: if you can evaluate AI-generated content—spot the subtle errors, question the confident-sounding nonsense, distinguish sound reasoning from plausible fluff—you become the person everyone needs in the room.

Complex problem-solving. The problems worth solving are the messy ones—competing stakeholders, incomplete information, tradeoffs that involve values. These are the problems that earn promotions and build reputations, precisely because they can't be automated.

Communication and influence. Every career breakthrough I've had came through persuading someone—a board, a team, a skeptical executive. When I was at Booz Allen Hamilton, I spent thirteen years advising the Department of Defense, NSA, NIST, and federal intelligence agencies—work that required not just technical knowledge but the ability to walk into a room full of senior officials and make a compelling case for a course of action, often one they hadn't considered. That skill—reading the room, adjusting your message on the fly, building the credibility that makes people say yes—is what carried me from government consulting to becoming a CISO at one of the largest non-profit health insurers in the country. AI can draft your talking points. It can help you refine your arguments. It cannot do the persuading for you.

Creativity and innovation. Not creativity in the artistic sense alone, but the ability to see what doesn't exist yet and imagine how it could. This is the "dreamer premium" from Chapter 11—and it's the skill most resistant to automation.

Emotional intelligence. Understanding what people actually feel, building trust in high-stakes situations, navigating the politics of organizational life—these become more valuable as routine cognitive work gets automated, because the remaining work is almost entirely relational.

Learning agility. The people who adapt fastest tend to thrive regardless of what changes. This is less a skill and more a practice—a habit of staying curious, uncomfortable, and willing to be a beginner again.

Depreciating skills:

- Routine information lookup (AI can find information faster)
- Basic analysis that follows standard patterns
- First-draft content generation
- Simple decision-making with clear criteria
- Memorized knowledge that's easily searched

This doesn't mean these skills become worthless—it means they become commoditized. The premium shifts elsewhere.

The T-Shape for an AI World

Career advisors have long recommended "T-shaped" professionals: deep expertise in one area (the vertical) plus broad capabilities across related areas (the horizontal). This model gets even more important in an AI world, with an addition.

The vertical: Deep domain expertise

AI can be a generalist. What it can't be is the person who truly understands a specific domain—its context, history, relationships, and unwritten rules. Deep expertise in a field remains valuable because it provides context AI lacks.

But here's the catch: the expertise needs to be genuine, not just credential-based. AI can match shallow expertise. It can't match deep understanding built through years of experience and reflection.

The horizontal: Broad connective capabilities

Cross-functional skills that let you work across boundaries—communication, collaboration, problem-solving, project management. These become more valuable as AI handles more routine work, because the remaining work requires more human coordination.

The new dimension: AI fluency

The T gets a third dimension: the ability to work effectively with AI across all your activities. This isn't technical expertise—it's the judgment to know when and how to leverage AI productively.

The most valuable professionals combine: deep domain expertise + broad collaborative skills + AI fluency. This combination is rare and increasingly powerful.

TRY THIS

Map your current skills against these three dimensions. Where is your depth? Where is your breadth? How strong is your AI fluency? What single investment would most improve your overall positioning?

Career Development Strategies

How do you actually develop your career in this environment? Here are practical strategies:

Invest continuously in learning.

Make learning a habit, not an occasional event. Your professional development didn't end with formal education.

Build AI fluency deliberately.

Use AI in your work regularly. Experiment. Develop judgment about when it helps and when it doesn't. You don't need to become a technical expert, but you do need to work effectively with AI tools.

Develop irreplaceable expertise.

Become genuinely expert in something—deep enough that your knowledge provides context and judgment AI lacks. This takes years, not months. Choose your area of depth deliberately, focusing on domains where human judgment remains essential.

Cultivate human skills.

Emotional intelligence, relationship-building, communication, ethical reasoning—these don't develop accidentally. Seek feedback, practice deliberately, and invest in growing capabilities that AI can't replicate.

Stay visible and connected.

In periods of change, opportunities often come through relationships. Stay connected to your professional community. Be known for your capabilities. Help others, and let others know how you can help.

Maintain optionality.

Don't bet your entire career on one specific role or company. Develop skills that transfer across contexts. Build a reputation beyond your current position. Keep options open as the landscape evolves.

Common Career Concerns

Here are concerns I hear frequently:

"I'm not technical. Will AI make me obsolete?"

AI fluency isn't the same as technical expertise. You don't need to code to work effectively with AI. What you need is the judgment to know how AI can help with your work and the skill to use it well. Many of the most valuable AI applications require domain expertise and human judgment, not technical depth.

"I'm already mid-career. Is it too late to adapt?"

Your experience gives you advantages—domain knowledge, professional relationships, contextual understanding that AI lacks. The challenge is combining that foundation with AI capabilities. Mid-career professionals who embrace AI often outperform younger colleagues who have AI fluency but lack domain depth.

"My field is being heavily automated. Should I change careers?"

Maybe, but probably not completely. More often, the answer is to shift within your field toward work that AI augments rather than replaces. The expertise you've built still has value—the question is how to deploy it differently.

"How do I know which skills to develop?"

Start with your current work. What parts could AI help with? What parts require your judgment and expertise? What would you be doing if AI handled the routine parts? Those answers point toward your development priorities.

The Human Premium

Here's the conviction I keep returning to throughout this book: in a world of artificial intelligence, authentic human intelligence becomes more valuable than ever.

When AI can generate adequate content on any topic, exceptional human insight stands out more. When AI handles routine interactions, genuine human connection becomes distinctive. When AI makes everyone's baseline competence higher, what differentiates people is the uniquely human contribution.

This "human premium" shows up in several ways:

Judgment and wisdom. AI provides information and analysis. Humans provide judgment about what matters and wisdom about how to act. These aren't skills AI is approaching.

Meaning and purpose. AI doesn't have purposes—it doesn't want anything. Humans bring meaning to work, setting direction that AI can help execute but can't originate.

Trust and relationships. People trust people. Organizations run on relationships that AI can support but can't replace.

Ethical reasoning. Navigating values, making difficult tradeoffs, acting with integrity—these remain human responsibilities.

The career implications: invest in becoming more genuinely human in your work, not less. The answer to AI isn't to become more machine-like. It's to become more distinctively human while leveraging AI for what machines do well.

> **THINK ABOUT IT**
>
> What do you bring to your work that no AI could replicate? What's distinctively human about your contribution? How

could you develop these qualities further?

Taking Agency

Perhaps the most important career advice I can offer: don't be passive.

Too many people wait—wait for their organization to tell them how to use AI, wait to see what happens to their industry, wait for clearer direction before acting. I've watched talented people get left behind not because they lacked ability, but because they waited for certainty that never came.

My own career pivot is proof that agency matters more than credentials. I hadn't written code since the 1980s. The idea of building software was as remote as my college programming courses. But rather than waiting to see how AI would affect my work, I sat down with an AI assistant and described an application I wanted to build. Three hours later I had a working prototype. By the end of the day, it was deployed to the cloud. The barrier I'd assumed was permanent—between "people who build software" and "everyone else"—simply dissolved. That didn't happen because I was technical. It happened because I was willing to try.

Waiting is a choice, and usually not a good one.

Take ownership of your development. Your organization may or may not invest in helping you adapt. Either way, your career is your responsibility. Invest in yourself even if no one else does.

Experiment proactively. Don't wait for permission to try AI in your work. Find ways to improve what you do. Learn what works and what doesn't. Become the person who understands how AI applies to your domain.

Share what you learn. Being known as someone who's adapting successfully creates opportunities. Help colleagues. Write about your experiences. Build a reputation as someone navigating change well.

Make deliberate choices. Think about where your field is heading, not just where it is now. Develop skills that will matter, not just skills that matter today. Position yourself for where things are going.

Stay curious. The landscape keeps changing. What's true today may not be true tomorrow. Stay engaged with developments. Keep learning. Remain adaptable.

The Long View

Career planning in an AI world requires holding two seemingly contradictory truths:

Things are changing faster than ever. What's impossible this year may be routine next year.

Fundamental human value endures. Despite all the change, what makes humans valuable—judgment, creativity, relationships, meaning—remains constant. These capabilities become more valuable, not less, as AI handles more routine work.

The practical implication: invest in both adaptability and depth. Build skills that are timeless while staying current with change. Develop the capacity to keep learning while building genuine expertise.

Your career is a decades-long journey, and AI is one of several major changes you'll navigate—probably not the last one that feels this disorienting. The professionals who thrive embrace change while building enduring capabilities. You can be one of them—if you start now rather than waiting for the dust to settle.

Chapter Summary

Key takeaways:

- Compete on human capabilities that complement AI, not capabilities that compete with it

- Build a portfolio of skills: deep expertise + broad collaboration + AI fluency
- Make learning a practice, not an event—your ability to adapt is your most durable career asset
- The "human premium"—judgment, meaning, relationships—increases as AI handles routine work
- Take agency in your career; don't wait for others to tell you how to adapt

A question to sit with:

What work do you do that you would keep doing even if AI could do it better? Why? Your answer points toward what gives your work meaning beyond mere output.

What's next: Part 5 shifts to the deeper questions—ethics, values, and what it means to live well in an AI-enabled world.

"In a world of artificial intelligence, authentic human intelligence is more valuable than ever."

Chapter 14: The Ethics of AI Use

I started building my AI assistant app after a two-hour conversation with an AI about the implications of AI privacy and security. It was one of those conversations that kept pulling me deeper. I'd noticed something that should have been obvious: everything about us is being recorded, captured, and archived. Products like Otter and Plaud record your meetings. Your phone tracks your location. Your email, your messages, your browsing—all captured, all stored, all potentially accessible to someone who isn't you.

So I asked the AI a question that I couldn't stop thinking about: What are the legal implications if someone recorded everything that went on around them, but stored it in a sort of digital consciousness that only they had access to?

Think about it. We already have organic consciousness—our brain records experiences, stores memories, processes them, and makes them available when we need them. What if a digital system did the same thing? What if an AI connected to your phone, your cloud storage, maybe eventually embedded in your body, captured everything you experienced and held it as an extension of your mind? Where does your consciousness end and the technology begin? Where is the boundary of *you*?

These aren't science fiction questions anymore. I've read enough science fiction about AI implants enhancing human capability to recognize that we're closer to that reality than most people realize. And the ethical questions that come with it are ones we haven't even begun to answer as a society.

That conversation started me on a journey to build a product that would mirror this problem—not to solve it, but to help me think through it. How do you secure something like this? How do you think about privacy when the boundaries between person and technology are dissolving?

This chapter is about what I've learned—not abstract philosophy, but practical ethical thinking born from actually building the technology and grappling with the consequences.

CHAPTER OVERVIEW

What you'll learn: - Ethical frameworks for thinking about AI use - Privacy, bias, authenticity, and accountability in practice - Your responsibilities as someone using AI - How to navigate the evolving ethical landscape

Why it matters: AI amplifies our capabilities; ethics guides how we use that amplification.

Reading time: About 18 minutes

Why Ethics Matters for AI Users

You might think ethics is someone else's concern—the domain of AI companies, policymakers, or academics. But every person who uses AI makes ethical choices, whether they realize it or not:

- What information do you share with AI systems?
- How do you use AI-generated content?
- What do you disclose about AI involvement in your work?
- How do you verify what AI tells you before acting on it?
- What boundaries do you maintain around AI use?

These aren't abstract questions. They're decisions you make regularly, often without realizing you're making them. The goal of this chapter is to help you make them more deliberately.

My own ethical thinking about AI didn't come from reading philosophy papers. It came from building things. From running a fifty-person pilot program where AI could pull external packages and execute system commands—and watching the security implications unfold in real time. From creating an AI assistant that ingests medical data, personal conversations, and twenty years of my own writing—and having to decide what protections that demands. From publishing books and having to answer Amazon's question about AI-generated content. Every one of these experiences forced me to think about ethics not in the abstract but in the specific.

Ethics isn't a constraint on effective AI use—it's part of effective AI use. Using AI without ethical consideration creates risks: to your reputation, relationships, and results. Thoughtful ethical practice makes AI use more sustainable and more valuable.

> **KEY POINT**
>
> Every AI user makes ethical choices. The question isn't whether to engage with ethics, but whether to engage thoughtfully.

A Framework for Thinking

Rather than prescribe rules, let me offer a framework for ethical thinking about AI use. This isn't comprehensive philosophy—it's practical guidance for everyday decisions.

I studied theology and ethics at Fuller Seminary, where I was usually the only businessperson in a room full of people training for ministry. That experience taught me something that applies directly to AI: ethical frameworks matter not because they give you easy answers, but because they help you ask better questions. The African pastor in my program who was trying to figure out how to grow bananas to feed his congregation and the corporate executive trying to figure out how to serve stakeholders ethically were wrestling with the same fundamental question: How do you act rightly when the path isn't clear?

Three questions to ask:

1. **Who is affected?** Your AI use affects more than just you. It may affect people whose data trained the AI, people who encounter AI-assisted output, people who compete with AI-augmented work, and people whose trust depends on your authenticity.

2. **What are the risks?** What could go wrong? What harms could result from this use of AI? What would happen if everyone used AI this way?

3. **What are my responsibilities?** What do I owe to others in this situation? What standards should guide my choices? What would a thoughtful, ethical person do?

Multiple ethical lenses:

Different ethical frameworks illuminate different considerations:

Consequences: What outcomes does this action produce? Does it create more benefit than harm?

Duties: What obligations do I have regardless of consequences? Are there things I shouldn't do even if they produce good outcomes?

Character: What kind of person am I becoming through this choice? Does this action reflect the values I want to embody?

Relationships: How does this affect trust and connection with others? Am I treating people as ends in themselves or merely as means?

You don't need to choose one framework. Drawing on multiple perspectives often produces better ethical reasoning than commitment to a single approach.

Privacy and the Boundaries of Self

One of the most immediate ethical considerations in AI use involves privacy—yours and others'. But the privacy question is deeper than most people realize.

I built my AI assistant to help me think through this. Into my app I pulled transcripts from meeting recordings, all of my medical data, context from my writings, emails, LinkedIn posts—essentially everything I could find about my own life. But here's the critical difference: I built it on a database that only I control, protected with advanced encryption, designed so it could be hosted on a user's personal cloud without any government or corporation ever accessing the data.

Then I experimented with something more radical: ambient listening. The app picks up conversation around me, transforms it into a transcript, tries to identify who's talking, but then converts it into something more like human memory—not exact word-for-word transcription, but context. What happened. What were the key ideas. Trying to replicate what happens in our brains rather than what happens in a database.

This raised the question I keep coming back to: If an AI records everything that goes on around me, remembers like a friend rather than a computer, and functions as a cognitive extension of my mind—is it part of me?

Right now, we tend to treat all digital data as not belonging to the individual. I think this is a significant problem. Data about us can be used to manipulate and control society. Businesses and governments are incentivized to use data to influence behavior and generate revenue. Both activities, as long as they provide broad value and recognize the worth of individual humans, can be positive. But what starts as a good idea with good intentions can quickly turn into something that restricts and exploits. The distance between corporate strategy and individual daily life makes it easy to lose sight of real human impact.

Your own privacy in practice:

When you interact with AI, you share information. That information may be stored, used for training, or accessible to others depending on the service and its policies.

Questions to consider: - What data am I sharing with this AI system? - What are the data retention and usage policies? - Could this data be combined with other information to reveal things I'd rather keep private? - Am I comfortable with how this information might be used?

Others' privacy:

You may share information about other people with AI systems. This raises additional questions:

- Do I have permission to share this information?
- Would the person be comfortable knowing I shared this?
- Am I protecting sensitive information appropriately?
- Could this information harm someone if misused?

I learned this personally through my "better husband" experiment, where I recorded conversations with my wife and asked AI for relationship advice (Chapter 9). The AI's advice was correct but not particularly enlightening—what mattered ethically was that I'd done the experiment with clear boundaries. My wife knew I was recording the entire time, even though we both mostly forgot about it. The ethical question wasn't whether the technology could record—of course it could. The question was whether I had the right to, and whether the person affected had given informed consent.

Practical guidance:

- Review privacy policies and data practices for AI services you use
- Avoid sharing highly sensitive information unless necessary and appropriate
- Consider whether you'd be comfortable if your AI interactions became public
- When in doubt, share less rather than more

- Remember that other people's data deserves the same protection you'd want for your own

TRY THIS

Review your recent AI interactions. What information have you shared? Are you comfortable with that data being stored and potentially used? Would you share the same information if it were a conversation with a stranger?

Bias and Fairness

AI systems can perpetuate and amplify biases. This isn't malice—it's a consequence of training on human-generated data that reflects human biases.

How bias appears:

- Language patterns that favor certain groups
- Assumptions embedded in responses
- Underrepresentation of some perspectives
- Stereotypes reflected in generated content

I encountered this in my own corporate analysis work. When I asked AI to analyze companies, it would reproduce the same analytical frameworks and assumptions that dominate business thinking—focusing on financial metrics and shareholder value while underweighting stakeholder impact, community effects, and ethical considerations. The AI wasn't being malicious. It was reflecting the bias of its training data, which overwhelmingly represents a particular worldview about what matters in business.

Your responsibilities:

- Be aware that AI outputs may reflect biases
- Review AI-generated content critically, especially when it involves or affects people
- Don't assume AI outputs are neutral or objective

- Be particularly careful when AI is used in decisions that affect people's opportunities

Practical guidance:

- When AI generates content about people or groups, examine it for assumptions and stereotypes
- Seek diverse perspectives rather than relying solely on AI
- Be especially cautious using AI in hiring, evaluation, or other high-stakes decisions
- If AI output seems biased, don't use it—generate alternatives or write it yourself

Authenticity and Transparency

AI raises fundamental questions about authenticity. When you present AI-assisted work as your own, what are your obligations?

I had to answer this question directly. Amazon requires a statement about AI-generated content when you publish a book. I asked Claude what it thought my answer should be, and it said my writing fell into the "AI-assisted" category—I didn't technically have to disclose AI involvement to Amazon.

But I chose to over-disclose rather than under-disclose. I was very explicit that AI created most of my graphics and my book covers, and I claimed some of my content was AI-created even though it used pre-existing content from me that AI helped me organize and iterate through. My reasoning was simple: Amazon and the rest of us are still trying to figure this out. I'd rather be transparent than exploit ambiguity in a system that hasn't caught up with the technology.

The authenticity spectrum:

At one end: using AI to generate something and presenting it as entirely your own creation with no disclosure.

At the other end: fully disclosing AI involvement in every interaction.

Most situations fall somewhere in between, and reasonable people can disagree about where to draw lines. The question I keep coming back to is: What's the difference between AI-generated content, AI-assisted content, and content that is purely mine? When I dictate my thoughts, have AI help me organize them, then edit the result extensively—whose words are they? When AI helps me brainstorm but I don't use any of its actual language—is that AI-assisted? The lines aren't clean.

Considerations:

Context matters. Using AI to draft an informal email probably doesn't require disclosure. Using AI to write a dissertation clearly does. The expectations and stakes of the context shape the obligation.

Relationship expectations. What do the people receiving your output reasonably expect? If they expect your personal voice and judgment, AI generation may violate that expectation even without explicit rules against it.

The substance of your contribution. Did you supply the ideas, judgment, and direction while AI helped with expression? Or did AI supply the substance while you merely polished? Your genuine contribution affects the authenticity question.

Practical guidance:

- When in doubt, disclose
- Err toward transparency rather than concealment
- Consider what reasonable people would expect in this context
- Ensure that work presented as yours reflects your genuine thought and judgment

THINK ABOUT IT

Where do you draw the line between legitimate AI assistance and inappropriate passing off AI work as your own? What factors influence where you draw that line?

Accountability

When AI is involved in work or decisions, accountability can become murky. Whose responsibility is it when things go wrong?

The accountability principle:

AI doesn't remove human responsibility—it shifts how that responsibility manifests. You remain accountable for:

- Choosing to use AI for this purpose
- The context and guidance you provide to AI
- Reviewing and accepting AI output
- Decisions made based on AI assistance
- Consequences that result from AI-assisted work

I saw this play out concretely in our developer pilot. AI coding tools could pull external packages and shell out code—powerful capabilities that also created real security risks. We had to embed industry security standards—OWASP, NIST, and HIPAA—directly into the AI's rules files, building guardrails into the tool itself. But the tools couldn't enforce judgment. A developer who accepted AI-generated code without reviewing it was still responsible for what that code did, regardless of where it came from.

The moral deflection trap:

A particular danger of AI is that it enables moral deflection—the temptation to use technology to avoid responsibility for harm.

Consider the classic deflections: "I didn't do it, you can't prove it, I did nothing wrong." Technology enables sophisticated versions: "The algorithm decided, not me." "The AI generated that, not me." "I'm just using the tool as designed."

But using AI doesn't remove your moral agency. If you use AI to produce something harmful, the harm doesn't disappear because a machine was involved. If you use AI to avoid dealing with difficult ethical questions, you've made an ethical choice—you just haven't acknowledged it.

The genuine ethical position isn't "the technology did it" but "I am responsible for what I create and release into the world, regardless of what tools I use to create it."

The Content Ethics Question

There's an ethical dimension to AI-generated content that goes beyond disclosure: the question of value.

If you use AI to generate content, are you creating something genuinely useful or are you generating slop for personal gain? There's a lot of AI-generated content on YouTube and other platforms that people use to drive revenue but that provides minimal value. Clickbait thumbnails over recycled ideas with AI narration—technically content, practically worthless.

Who should police the slop? Should platforms? Should viewers police it through their own discretion?

What I find genuinely unethical is the use of AI to create low-value content for purely political or economic gain—content designed not to inform or help but to manipulate attention for profit. In a free society, much of this we can let the consumer decide. People are smarter than we give them credit for, and most AI slop fails on its own lack of merit.

We get into much more difficult ethical territory when AI is used to manipulate people at scale, malign individuals, or intentionally cause harm. I was at the RSA cybersecurity conference in 2019 and saw a researcher present on organized bot networks—systems where people could pay to have automated accounts click on their posts, inflate their metrics, and manufacture the appearance of popularity. The researcher's finding: the primary paying customers of these networks were celebrities and politicians. That was before generative AI made it possible to create not just fake engagement but fake content at industrial scale.

The same tools that let me write and publish a book in weeks could let someone generate hundreds of fake books, flood a platform with manufactured reviews, or produce an endless stream of plausible-sounding misinformation. The technology doesn't distinguish between creation and manipulation. The ethics have to come from the person using it.

Building Ethical Practice

Rather than memorizing rules, build habits that support ethical AI use.

The price of principle:

Here's an uncomfortable truth: genuine ethical practice comes with a cost. If doing the right thing with AI were always the easy, efficient, profitable thing, everyone would do it. The reason ethical practice matters is precisely because it sometimes means choosing a harder path.

I experienced this with my Amazon disclosure decision. I could have truthfully said my books weren't AI-generated—Claude confirmed it. That would have been easier and might have avoided any stigma around AI involvement. Instead, I chose to be explicit about AI's role because I believed transparency mattered more than convenience, even when the rules didn't require it.

If your ethical AI practices never cost you anything—never slow you down, never reduce efficiency, never mean declining an opportunity—you might ask whether you're really making ethical choices or just following rules that happen to align with your interests.

Regular reflection:

Periodically review your AI use. Are you comfortable with how you're using it? Would you be comfortable if your use were visible to others? Are there practices you should change?

Staying informed:

Ethics evolves with capabilities and social understanding. Stay current with thinking about AI ethics. Be willing to update your practices as understanding develops.

Seeking feedback:

Others may notice ethical concerns you miss. Be open to feedback about your AI use. Engage with people who raise concerns rather than dismissing them.

Starting conservative:

When uncertain, choose the more cautious path. You can always expand your use as you develop better judgment. It's harder to repair damage from aggressive choices.

The Balance: Guardrails and Innovation

One of the most important challenges from an ethics perspective is maintaining a balance between ensuring proper societal guardrails around the technology and encouraging experimentation and innovation.

This is going to be a continually evolving journey. Right now, I think there's more hype and misunderstanding about AI than there is a solid foundation for good public policy. The technology is moving faster than our collective ability to understand it, much less regulate it wisely.

My own approach has been to experiment extensively while maintaining clear ethical boundaries. Building my AI assistant app taught me more about AI privacy than any policy paper could—because I had to make actual decisions about encryption, data access, ambient recording, and memory systems. Publishing books with AI assistance forced me to think about disclosure in concrete terms rather than abstract ones. Running a developer pilot with fifty people showed me where AI creates real security risks and where the fears are overblown.

That's part of why I wrote this book—to help people understand AI and how they can use it in their lives effectively and ethically. Not because I have all the answers, but because I believe informed individuals making thoughtful choices is a better foundation for ethical AI use than waiting for perfect policy.

A Personal Ethics Statement

Consider developing your own ethics statement for AI use—a brief articulation of the principles that guide your practice.

Elements might include: - What purposes you will and won't use AI for - How you handle disclosure and transparency - What verification practices you maintain - How you think about impact on others - Where you draw lines and why

This doesn't need to be public or formal. Its value is in clarifying your own thinking and creating a reference point for decisions.

> **TRY THIS**
>
> Draft a brief personal ethics statement for your AI use. What principles guide your practice? Where do you draw lines? Having a written statement helps you make consistent decisions and recognize when circumstances challenge your principles.

Chapter Summary

Key takeaways:

- Every AI user makes ethical choices, whether they realize it or not
- Privacy is deeper than data policies—it touches questions of consciousness, identity, and what constitutes the self in a digital age
- Transparency about AI use builds trust; when in doubt, over-disclose rather than under-disclose

- You remain accountable for AI-assisted work—"the AI did it" is never a defense
- The ethics of AI content aren't just about disclosure but about value—are you creating something genuinely useful?
- Balance societal guardrails with room for experimentation; this is an evolving journey, not a destination
- Informed individuals making thoughtful choices is the best foundation for ethical AI use

What's next: Chapter 15 moves beyond compliance to aspiration—exploring the values that can guide AI use toward genuine human flourishing.

"AI amplifies our ability to act. Ethics is about whether that action serves something larger than ourselves."

Chapter 15: Values and Human Flourishing

The previous chapter offered frameworks for ethical thinking about AI. But frameworks only take you so far. At some point, you encounter questions that can't be resolved by applying rules or calculating consequences.

I've spent a lot of time wrestling with these deeper questions—not just professionally, but personally. What grounds human dignity? What makes life meaningful? What are we ultimately aiming for when we talk about "good" AI use?

My own thinking is shaped by the Christian tradition—particularly thinkers like C.S. Lewis, Francis Schaeffer, and Timothy Keller. I don't assume readers share that tradition. But I've found that being transparent about where my values come from is more honest than pretending I'm speaking from nowhere. And I've found that insights from my tradition often resonate with people who come from different starting points.

This chapter explores the deeper questions behind ethics—not to prescribe a single answer, but to help you think about your own. I'll share how I think about these questions, drawing on resources that have shaped me, while inviting you to engage from wherever you stand.

Questions like: - What is a human being, and what does that mean for how we relate to AI? - What makes life meaningful, and can AI contribute to or detract from that meaning? - What are we ultimately aiming for when we talk about "good" AI use?

These aren't questions ethics frameworks answer. They're questions about values—about what we believe regarding human nature, purpose, and flourishing.

> **CHAPTER OVERVIEW**
>
> **What you'll learn:** - The limits of ethics frameworks and why values matter - How different traditions understand human dignity and purpose - The relationship between technology and human flourishing - How to develop a coherent approach to AI grounded in your deepest values
>
> **Why it matters:** What you believe about human nature shapes how you use AI.
>
> **Reading time:** About 20 minutes

The Limits of Frameworks

I ran into the limits of frameworks in my own work. When we automated our security operations—the transformation I described in Chapter 1—the efficiency gains were extraordinary. But at one point, I had to make a decision that no framework could resolve for me.

We had the capability to automate even more of the alert-handling process, pushing AI-driven triage further into the workflow. The metrics said we should. Response times would improve. False positive rates would drop. Every quantitative measure pointed in the same direction: automate more.

But I hesitated. The cases we were considering automating were the ones where my junior analysts were learning the most. The messy, ambiguous cases—the ones that weren't clearly malicious or clearly benign—were exactly where analysts developed the judgment that would make them senior analysts someday. Automating those cases would improve our metrics today while hollowing out the development pipeline for tomorrow. We'd be more efficient and less resilient.

No utilitarian calculation could resolve this cleanly. No rule-based framework gave a clear answer. The decision required something deeper—a conviction about what I owed to the people on my team, not just the organization's performance metrics. I chose to keep those cases in human hands, accepting slightly lower efficiency numbers in exchange for developing the people who would eventually lead our security program.

That experience taught me what this chapter explores: ethics frameworks are useful tools, but they have significant limitations.

Frameworks require inputs they don't supply.

A utilitarian framework tells you to maximize good outcomes—but doesn't tell you what counts as "good." A virtue framework tells you to cultivate excellent character—but doesn't specify which virtues to prioritize. Every framework depends on value assumptions it cannot justify from within itself.

Frameworks can't resolve deep disagreements.

When people disagree about fundamental values—not just how to apply them, but what they are—frameworks provide no mechanism for resolution. They're useful for people who share underlying values; they're useless for bridging fundamentally different worldviews.

Frameworks focus on decisions, not formation.

Most ethics frameworks help you decide what to do in specific situations. They're less helpful for the broader question of who you're becoming over time. Character development—the shape of your life—isn't reducible to a series of correct decisions.

Frameworks don't address meaning.

The question "Is this decision ethical?" differs from "What makes life meaningful?" Ethics frameworks address the former; they have little to say about the latter. Yet questions of meaning are central to how we relate to technology.

This isn't an argument against ethics frameworks—they're valuable tools. It's an argument that frameworks alone aren't sufficient. Deeper questions require deeper resources.

KEY POINT

Ethics frameworks tell you how to make decisions. Values tell you what kind of person to be and what kind of life to live.

Human Dignity

Most thoughtful approaches to AI ethics converge on human dignity as foundational. But what grounds that dignity, and what does it mean?

Human beings have inherent worth.

Not worth derived from productivity, utility, or capability. Not worth that can be measured against or compared to AI capability. Inherent worth that exists simply by virtue of being human.

This has practical implications: AI should serve humans, not the reverse. Humans should never be reduced to inputs, resources, or problems to be optimized. The convenience of AI systems should never come at the cost of treating people as less than fully human.

Humans are not reducible to their capabilities.

If human value derived from what we can do, AI would indeed be threatening—machines can do many things better than us. But human worth doesn't derive from capability. A person with disabilities is no less valuable than an athlete. A sleeping child is no less valuable than a productive adult.

This means AI "replacing" human capabilities doesn't diminish human worth. It might change what we do, but it doesn't change who we are.

Humans have agency and responsibility.

To be human is to make choices—and to be accountable for them. AI cannot take responsibility in any meaningful sense. This means humans must remain responsible for AI-assisted decisions and actions. Delegating execution is fine; abdicating responsibility is not.

What Makes Life Meaningful?

If technology is supposed to serve human flourishing, we need some idea of what flourishing involves.

Relationships and love.

Most accounts of meaningful life put relationships near the center. Love for family, friends, communities—being known and knowing others. Technology that strengthens relationships contributes to flourishing; technology that substitutes for them may not.

Consider: Does your AI use strengthen your human relationships, or does it become a substitute for them? Are you more connected or more isolated because of how you use AI?

Purposeful work.

Work isn't just economic activity. At its best, work involves applying your capabilities to serve others and contribute to something larger than yourself. Meaningful work provides not just income but identity and purpose.

Consider: Does AI make your work more meaningful, or does it reduce work to mere production? Are you doing work that matters, or just generating output?

Growth and development.

Humans flourish when learning, growing, developing capabilities. Stagnation leads to withering, not flourishing. Challenge and struggle, appropriately sized, contribute to growth.

Consider: Does AI use support your growth, or does it shortcut development you need? Are you becoming more capable over time, or are you outsourcing capabilities you should be developing?

Connection to something larger.

Most people need a sense that their life connects to something beyond themselves—family, community, tradition, purpose, transcendence. Pure individualism rarely produces flourishing.

Consider: Does AI use connect you to larger purposes, or does it feed isolation and individualism?

THINK ABOUT IT

What makes your life meaningful? When do you feel most alive, most yourself, most fulfilled? How does AI use relate to those moments—does it contribute to them or compete with them?

Technology in Service of Human Good

Throughout history, technology has been a double-edged sword—capable of serving human flourishing and capable of undermining it. The same is true of AI.

Technology as tool, not master.

Tools extend human capability. They should remain under human direction, serving human purposes. When tools start directing human activity rather than extending it, something has gone wrong.

This requires deliberate attention. AI systems are designed to be engaging, to keep you interacting. Without intention, you may find technology using you rather than the reverse.

The trust dimension.

We live in an era of eroding trust. Research consistently shows declining confidence in institutions—government, media, corporations, even nonprofits. In this environment, how we use AI matters not just for individual outcomes but for the social fabric.

AI deployed in ways that manipulate, deceive, or exploit accelerates the trust crisis. AI used transparently, honestly, and in genuine service of others can help rebuild trust. The question isn't just "Is this AI use effective?" but "Does this AI use build or erode the trust that makes society function?"

Consider: Would the people affected by your AI use trust you more or less if they understood exactly how you're using it?

Technology as amplifier.

Technology amplifies human intentions and capabilities. Fire can cook food or destroy homes. AI can enhance productivity or enable manipulation. The technology itself is neutral; human direction determines outcomes.

This means the ethics of AI use depends substantially on what you're using it for. The same capability can serve good or ill depending on purpose.

Technology and human limits.

Technology sometimes promises to transcend human limitations—and sometimes delivers on that promise. But not all limitations are problems to be solved. Some limitations are features, not bugs—constraints that shape meaningful human experience.

Consider death and suffering. Technology can reduce unnecessary suffering—a clear good. But it cannot eliminate the fundamental human experience of vulnerability, limitation, and mortality. Nor should we necessarily want it to. These limitations shape what makes life precious.

A Values Framework

Without prescribing a specific tradition, here are values that many thoughtful people bring to AI use:

Human dignity. People have inherent worth not derived from utility. This worth demands respect in how AI treats people and how we use AI regarding people.

Truth. Reality matters; deception is harmful. AI should support truth-seeking, not enable manipulation or the spread of falsehood.

Justice. Fair dealing with others matters. AI should not be used to exploit, manipulate, or take unfair advantage.

Stewardship. We're responsible for how we use power and capability. AI amplifies our power; responsible stewardship becomes more important, not less.

Humility. We don't know everything; our judgment is fallible. AI confidence doesn't mean human certainty. Maintaining appropriate humility about what we know and can do remains important.

Love. Genuine concern for others' good matters. Technology use that treats others merely as means rather than ends violates this fundamental value.

These values don't resolve every question. But they provide orientation—a direction for thinking rather than a predetermined destination.

The Leadership of Influence

Even if you don't hold a leadership title, your AI use influences others. In organizations, among colleagues, in families—how you use AI shapes what others see as normal and acceptable.

Leaders drive culture, culture drives behavior, behavior drives results.

This principle applies to AI adoption at every level. How leaders use AI—transparently or secretly, ethically or expeditiously, thoughtfully or carelessly—shapes organizational culture around AI. That culture shapes how others behave. Those behaviors produce results.

This means your AI practices have ripple effects beyond your immediate work. If you use AI ethically and transparently, you normalize ethical AI use. If you cut corners or hide AI involvement, you normalize those practices too.

The servant leadership principle.

One enduring insight from leadership wisdom: the most effective and ethical leaders put the mission first, the team second, and themselves last. This ordering applies to AI use:

- **Mission first:** Use AI to serve the genuine purpose of your work, not just personal convenience
- **Team/community second:** Consider how your AI use affects colleagues, customers, and those you serve
- **Self last:** Personal efficiency gains matter least when they conflict with larger purposes

This doesn't mean ignoring your own interests. It means ordering priorities correctly. When personal convenience conflicts with serving others well, the servant-leadership model prioritizes others.

> **THINK ABOUT IT**
>
> How does your AI use affect people beyond yourself? If you lead others—formally or informally—what norms are you establishing about ethical AI practice?

Questions AI Raises

AI makes certain value questions more urgent. Consider:

What is a person?

If AI can simulate human conversation convincingly, what distinguishes genuine human interaction from simulation? What makes human consciousness, feeling, and experience different from information processing?

These aren't new questions, but AI makes them more pressing. Your answer shapes how you relate to AI and what boundaries you maintain.

What is human work?

If AI can do knowledge work faster and cheaper than humans, what is the purpose of human work? Is it primarily economic—producing goods and services? Or does it serve other purposes—developing capability, contributing to community, expressing creativity?

Your answer shapes how you think about AI in the workplace and what you think humans should do that AI shouldn't.

What is genuine relationship?

If AI can provide conversation, support, and even apparent emotional connection, what distinguishes genuine human relationship? What do we miss when we substitute AI interaction for human connection?

Your answer shapes what kinds of AI use you embrace and which you avoid.

What is authentic creativity?

If AI can generate art, music, and writing, what makes human creativity valuable? Is it the output itself, or the human process of creation? Does AI-assisted creation differ meaningfully from AI generation?

Your answer shapes how you think about creative work in an AI world.

Wisdom Traditions and What They Offer

Different wisdom traditions offer resources for thinking about these questions. Let me share what I've found valuable from mine, while acknowledging that readers will bring their own sources of wisdom.

The question of presuppositions.

Francis Schaeffer argued that presuppositions—the assumptions we bring to any question—shape everything that follows. We don't approach AI ethics from a neutral position. We bring beliefs about human nature, about reality, about what matters. Being honest about those presuppositions is more intellectually rigorous than pretending we don't have them.

What presuppositions do you bring to questions about AI? About human nature? About what makes life meaningful? Naming them clarifies your thinking.

The reality of objective value.

C.S. Lewis, in *The Abolition of Man*, warned about what happens when we reject the idea of objective value—what he called "the Tao," the moral law that exists across cultures. If there's no objective standard for human dignity, then "human dignity" becomes merely what those in power decide it means. Without a moral reality outside ourselves, we don't free ourselves from external constraints—we simply hand that power to whoever can shape values on their own terms.

This has direct implications for AI. If human dignity is merely a social construct, then AI systems that optimize for engagement, profit, or efficiency have no real obligation to respect it. But if human dignity is objectively real—if "there are no ordinary people," as Lewis wrote, and "you have never talked to a mere mortal"—then AI must be designed and used in ways that honor that reality.

The danger of idolatry.

Timothy Keller's insight about idolatry—making good things into ultimate things—applies directly to technology. Technology, efficiency, productivity, data—these are goods. But when they become ultimate concerns, they distort everything else. When we optimize for efficiency at the cost of relationships, or pursue productivity at the expense of presence, we've made a good thing into an idol.

AI makes this temptation more acute. The promise of doing more, knowing more, producing more can easily become the ultimate goal rather than a tool serving genuinely ultimate purposes.

What other traditions offer.

I learn from my tradition, but I also learn from others:

- **Humanist traditions** rightly emphasize human reason, creativity, and agency as grounds for dignity
- **Virtue traditions** correctly focus on character formation over rule-following
- **Contemplative traditions** wisely warn against the tyranny of busyness and distraction
- **Other religious traditions** offer their own rich resources for thinking about human nature and technology

You don't need to share my tradition to benefit from its insights—just as I benefit from insights in traditions I don't fully share. What matters is engaging seriously with the deep questions and bringing resources that help you think clearly.

No matter how you approach this, AI brings us back to ultimate questions: What is good? Is there one moral law, or does society determine what is right? What does it mean to be human and live well in the world as it actually is? What we decide will determine how we use AI to enhance, control, or subvert human flourishing.

THINK ABOUT IT

What wisdom traditions have shaped your values? What do those traditions say about human nature, human dignity, and technology? How might their insights inform your AI use?

Developing Your Approach

How do you develop a coherent approach to AI grounded in your deepest values?

Know what you believe.

Clarify your own views on human dignity, meaning, purpose, and flourishing. Not just intellectually—what do you actually live by? What would you sacrifice for? What gives your life meaning?

Connect beliefs to practice.

Think through how your values apply to specific AI questions. If you believe human relationships are central to flourishing, what does that mean for AI use that might substitute for relationship? If you value truth, what does that mean for AI outputs you share with others?

Maintain integrity.

Aim for consistency between your stated values and your actual practice. We all fall short, but the gap between professed values and lived practice should trouble us. AI use that contradicts your core values undermines integrity regardless of whether anyone notices.

Stay open to growth.

Your understanding of values and their application will develop over time. New experiences, better understanding, encountering different perspectives—all can refine your thinking. Hold your conclusions firmly enough to guide action, loosely enough to allow growth.

Engage with others.

Values aren't purely individual—they're shaped by community, tradition, and dialogue. Engage with others about AI and ethics. Learn from different perspectives. Allow your thinking to be challenged and refined.

The Ultimate Questions

At the deepest level, how you relate to AI depends on how you answer questions about human existence:

What are human beings? Biological machines? Souls in bodies? Meaning-making creatures? Something else?

What gives life meaning? Achievement? Relationship? Pleasure? Service? Transcendence?

What is the good life? Success? Happiness? Virtue? Love? Holiness?

What happens when we die? Nothing? Something? Does it matter?

These questions might seem far from practical AI advice. But they actually determine the practical advice. If humans are just biological machines, AI that exceeds human capability naturally takes over. If humans have inherent dignity that transcends capability, the calculus changes entirely.

You don't need to resolve every ultimate question to use AI wisely. But knowing that these questions matter—and that your answers shape your practice—is part of thoughtful engagement with AI.

Chapter Summary

Key takeaways:

- Ethics frameworks are useful but limited; deeper values matter
- Human dignity—inherent worth not derived from capability—is foundational
- Flourishing involves relationship, purposeful work, growth, and connection to larger meaning
- Different wisdom traditions offer resources for thinking about AI and human purpose

- Developing a coherent approach requires connecting your deepest values to your practice

  A question to sit with:

  If you could give AI any set of values to optimize for, what would you choose? And what does your answer reveal about what you actually believe matters most?

What's next: Chapter 16 concludes the book with practical wisdom for living well with AI—bringing together everything we've explored into guidance for everyday life.

"What you believe about human nature shapes how you use AI. The deepest questions matter most."

Chapter 16: Living Well With AI

We've covered a lot of ground in this book—what AI is and isn't, how to work with it effectively, the practical applications, the implications for work and careers, and the deeper ethical questions. But books like this can leave you with information without wisdom, techniques without integration, knowledge without a coherent approach to living.

This final chapter is about integration. How do you take everything we've explored and weave it into a life that's genuinely good—not just productive, not just efficient, but flourishing? How do you live well with AI?

CHAPTER OVERVIEW

What you'll learn: - How to integrate AI thoughtfully into your life - Principles for maintaining healthy balance - The examined life in an AI age - A vision for human-AI partnership

Why it matters: The goal isn't optimal AI use. It's a good life. AI is one factor among many.

Reading time: About 15 minutes

What I Almost Got Wrong

Before we get to principles, let me tell you about something that almost went badly.

When I first discovered what AI could do, I went all in. I wanted to fully understand it, including the opportunities, risks, and pitfalls. Every task that could involve AI did involve AI. Research, writing, analysis, planning, communication—AI became my constant companion. I learned a tremendous amount about the technology, how it could be used, privacy and security concerns, and how it could be a force multiplier in my productivity.

For a few months, I was more productive than I'd ever been. Output soared. I was doing more in less time, tackling projects I'd previously avoided, generating work product at a pace that seemed almost unfair.

Then I noticed something troubling.

Using AI and using AI effectively were two different things. When faced with a complex problem, my first instinct was to ask AI rather than wrestle with it myself. The struggle that develops insight was being shortcut before it could do its work. It takes both deep experience and context augmented by AI to create the best results. I found the optimal approach was to struggle with AI augmenting and enhancing my thought process, not replacing it.

I also found that relying on AI for writing results in sounding too generic and losing your impact. When overusing AI, I found the voice I'd developed over decades was being smoothed into something that read fine but didn't sound like me. After my wife, a nurse, came home with a story about a hospital manager who sent out a Nurses Week email obviously written by AI, I understood the danger more viscerally. The staff found the email disingenuous. An email that was supposed to celebrate nurses turned into just more corporate junk mail at best and exposed the insensitivity of leadership at worst.

And the relationships that matter most were getting the leftover attention. It's easy to be "always on" with AI assistance—but always on means always distracted, always partially present, always somewhere other than here. Productivity has a purpose: create value that impacts family, friends, colleagues, and society around us—not an end in itself. With the paradigm change that AI brings, relationships are more important than ever for true value creation in our lives.

I had to pull back. Not abandon AI—that would be foolish—but establish boundaries. Certain kinds of thinking I do myself, even when AI could help. Certain writing stays entirely mine. Certain times are AI-free, not because AI isn't useful but because something else matters more.

The insight that stuck with me: doing less can drive better results. Not less AI, necessarily, but less *unexamined* AI. Quality over quantity. Presence over productivity. Being effective at what matters over being efficient at everything.

This chapter is about that balance—how to integrate AI into a life that's genuinely good, not just impressively productive.

Beyond Productivity

Let's start with something that might seem counterintuitive after a book full of practical AI techniques: productivity isn't the point.

Yes, AI can make you more productive. Yes, that matters. But productivity is a means, not an end. The question "How can I be more productive?" eventually leads to "Productive toward what?"

If increased productivity just means more output without more meaning, more activity without more fulfillment, more efficiency without more life—then what have you gained?

The goal isn't to use AI optimally. The goal is to live well. AI is one tool among many that might help or hinder that deeper aim.

This framing changes how you approach AI: - Instead of "How can I use AI more?" ask "How can I use AI better for what actually matters?" - Instead of "Am I maximizing AI capability?" ask "Is AI serving my actual purposes?" - Instead of "What else can AI do?" ask "What should AI do—and what should I do myself?"

> **KEY POINT**
>
> The examined life asks not just "How can I use AI?" but "What life am I building, and how does AI fit?"

Principles for Integration

Here are principles that guide thoughtful AI integration:

Intentionality over default.

Don't just use AI because it's there. Choose deliberately when AI serves your purposes and when it doesn't. Default to not using AI; adopt it when there's a clear reason.

This means sometimes declining to use AI even when it would be faster or easier. Speed and ease aren't always what matters most.

Enhancement over replacement.

Use AI to enhance your capabilities, not replace them. The goal is becoming more effective, not becoming dependent. If you couldn't do your work without AI, that's a warning sign.

Periodically do things without AI assistance—not to prove a point, but to maintain your own capabilities and perspective.

Boundaries over blur.

Maintain clear boundaries around AI use. Know when you're using AI and when you're not. Don't let AI quietly infiltrate every corner of your life.

This might mean designated AI-free times, places, or activities. It might mean reviewing your AI use periodically to ensure it remains intentional.

Relationship over efficiency.

Some things are more important than efficiency—particularly human relationships. Don't let AI use erode genuine connection with other people.

Be present with people. Have conversations without distraction. Maintain relationships through direct engagement, not AI-mediated communication.

Depth over breadth.

AI can help you do more things. But doing more things isn't always better. Sometimes depth in fewer areas produces a richer life than shallow engagement across many.

Use AI to go deeper, not just wider. Focus on what matters most rather than spreading attention everywhere.

The Examined AI Life

Socrates famously said the unexamined life is not worth living. In an AI age, we might add: the unexamined AI use is not worth having.

Regular reflection:

Periodically examine your AI use: - What am I using AI for? - Is this use serving my actual goals? - Am I becoming more capable or less? - Is AI enhancing my life or just filling it? - What would I change if I were starting fresh?

Honest assessment:

Be honest with yourself about what AI use is actually doing: - Are you using AI, or is AI using you? - Is this making you better at what matters? - Are you outsourcing things you should be developing? - Is AI serving your values or eroding them?

Course correction:

Be willing to change based on what reflection reveals. If AI use isn't serving you well, adjust. The goal isn't consistent AI use—it's a good life.

Maintaining Human Connection

One risk of AI integration is erosion of human connection. AI is always available, never tired, never impatient. It's easy to let AI substitute for human interaction, especially difficult human interaction.

This would be a mistake. Human relationships are central to flourishing. AI can support those relationships; it shouldn't replace them.

Practical guidance:

Prioritize presence. When you're with people, be with them. Don't let AI (or any technology) fragment your attention.

Choose humans for human things. For emotional support, deep conversation, genuine advice, real connection—choose humans. AI can provide information and even surface-level support; it cannot provide genuine human relationship.

Use AI to enhance relationships. AI can help you prepare for conversations, remember important details, find good gifts. Use it to be better in relationships, not to avoid them.

Maintain unmediated connection. Some conversations shouldn't be AI-assisted. Some messages should be entirely yours. Some moments should be purely human.

> **THINK ABOUT IT**
>
> How has your use of AI affected your human relationships? Are you more connected or less? More present or more distracted? What would the people who matter most to you say?

The Dangers of Dependence

AI can become a crutch that weakens what it supports. Consider:

Cognitive dependence. If you always rely on AI to think through problems, your own thinking may atrophy. The goal is augmentation, not substitution.

Creative dependence. If AI always starts your creative work, you may lose the capacity to face blank pages. The struggle of creation develops capabilities that shortcuts don't.

Social dependence. If you rely on AI for drafting messages, generating responses, or structuring communication, you may lose the capacity for unmediated human expression.

Emotional dependence. Some people develop quasi-relationships with AI assistants. This isn't the same as human relationship and may interfere with developing genuine connections.

The solution isn't avoiding AI. It's using AI intentionally while maintaining your own capabilities—and regularly exercising those capabilities without AI assistance.

A Balanced Approach

Balance in AI use means:

Using AI where it genuinely helps. AI offers real value. Don't avoid it out of misplaced principle. Let it help you be more effective at what matters.

Preserving what matters. Some human experiences have value that AI involvement would diminish. Preserve those experiences even when AI could "help."

Maintaining capabilities. Use AI without becoming dependent. Keep your own skills sharp. Know you could function without AI if needed.

Staying connected. Prioritize human relationships. Be present with people. Don't let AI substitute for genuine connection.

Living your values. Let your deepest values guide your AI use, not just convenience or efficiency.

This balance isn't a formula. It's ongoing judgment, informed by attention to what's actually happening in your life.

What AI Cannot Provide

A clear-eyed view of AI includes knowing what it cannot provide:

Meaning. AI has no sense of meaning or purpose. It doesn't experience its existence as meaningful. Meaning is something humans bring to life—AI can't supply it.

Love. AI can simulate care but cannot love. Genuine concern for another's well-being—willing sacrifice, patient endurance, authentic joy in another's flourishing—these remain human.

Wisdom. AI has information and patterns. Wisdom—knowing how to live well, understanding what matters, having judgment shaped by experience and reflection—this is human.

Presence. Being truly present with another person—fully attending, genuinely engaging—requires consciousness AI doesn't possess.

Purpose. AI has no purposes of its own. It doesn't want anything, aim at anything, care about anything. Human purposes direct AI; AI cannot supply purposes.

Understanding these limits helps you know where AI fits and where it doesn't. AI is extraordinarily capable within its domain. It's not capable of providing what makes human life worthwhile.

The Long View

Consider your relationship with AI over your lifetime:

AI capabilities will grow. What seems impressive now will seem primitive in a decade. The specific tools and techniques matter less than the principles of engagement.

Your needs will change. Different life stages bring different needs. How you use AI in your twenties will differ from how you use it at fifty. Stay flexible.

What matters most remains constant. Despite all the change, what makes life good—love, meaning, growth, contribution—doesn't change. Technology serves those constants; it doesn't replace them.

Your choices shape your life. You're not a passive recipient of technological change. You choose how to engage with AI, what role it plays, what boundaries you maintain. Those choices shape the life you build.

A Vision for Partnership

At its best, human-AI partnership could look like this:

AI handles the routine so humans can focus on what requires human judgment, creativity, and connection. The mundane work gets done; the meaningful work gets more attention.

AI extends human capability rather than replacing it. People do more than they could alone, but they remain the agents—thinking, choosing, taking responsibility.

AI supports human flourishing by removing barriers, enabling learning, connecting people, and creating opportunity. Technology serves human good rather than human good being sacrificed to technological progress.

Humans maintain wisdom and direction while AI provides capability and scale. The partnership combines machine ability with human purpose.

Values guide development so AI systems reflect what we care about rather than undermining it. Ethics isn't an afterthought but integral to how AI is built and used.

This vision requires intentional effort. It won't happen automatically. But it's possible—if enough people engage with AI thoughtfully rather than passively.

An Invitation

This book has offered information, techniques, frameworks, and principles. But ultimately, you have to decide how to live.

AI will continue developing. The specific advice in this book will need updating. But the fundamental questions remain:

What kind of life do you want to build? What role should AI play in that life? What matters enough to protect from technological encroachment? What opportunities does AI create that are worth pursuing?

These are your questions to answer. No book can answer them for you.

My invitation: engage with AI thoughtfully. Use it where it genuinely serves your purposes. Maintain what matters regardless of efficiency gains. Build a life you're proud of—one where AI is a useful tool, not an end in itself.

The technology will keep changing. Your values, developed and lived with integrity, will guide you through the changes.

> **A question to sit with:**
>
> A year from now, how will you know if you've integrated AI well into your life? What will be different—and what will have stayed the same that matters?

A Final Word

We live in a remarkable time. AI capabilities that seemed like science fiction are becoming daily reality. The possibilities are genuine; so are the risks.

But technology never determines outcomes. Human choices do. Your choices about how to engage with AI matter—for you, for the people around you, for the kind of world we build together.

I've tried to offer something useful: clear understanding of what AI is and how it works, practical guidance for using it effectively, honest assessment of its implications, and thoughtful engagement with the deeper questions.

What you do with it is up to you.

Whatever you choose, I hope you build a life rich with meaning, deep in relationship, and aligned with your truest values. AI can serve that life. But only you can live it.

"The dreamers will always have jobs—AI isn't replacing vision and big-picture thinking. And meaning? That remains, as it always has been, a human domain."

Glossary of AI Terms

This glossary provides non-technical definitions of terms used throughout this book. The goal is clarity for everyday readers, not technical precision.

A

Agentic AI – AI systems that can take actions autonomously toward a goal, making decisions along the way rather than just responding to single prompts. An agentic AI might research a topic, draft a document, revise based on feedback, and format the final result—all without step-by-step human direction.

AI (Artificial Intelligence) – Computer systems designed to perform tasks that typically require human intelligence, such as understanding language, recognizing patterns, and making decisions. In this book, "AI" primarily refers to large language models and related systems that can engage in conversation and generate content.

AI Assistant – An AI system designed to help users accomplish tasks through natural language interaction. Examples include ChatGPT, Claude, and similar tools. Also sometimes called "AI chatbots" or "AI agents."

Algorithm – A set of rules or instructions that a computer follows to complete a task. In AI, algorithms determine how the system processes input and generates output.

Autonomy – The degree to which an AI system operates independently versus requiring human direction. Higher autonomy means more independent action; lower autonomy means more human control.

Autonomy Spectrum – A framework for understanding the range of AI involvement in tasks, from fully human-directed (AI as a simple tool) to fully autonomous (AI acting independently). Most effective AI use falls somewhere in the middle, with humans and AI sharing responsibility at different levels.

B

Bias – Systematic patterns in AI output that favor certain perspectives, groups, or outcomes over others. Bias typically reflects patterns in the data used to train the AI system.

C

Chatbot – An AI program designed to simulate conversation with human users. Modern AI chatbots can handle complex conversations across many topics.

Context – The background information provided to an AI system that helps it understand what you're asking and respond appropriately. Good context typically includes who you are, what you're trying to accomplish, and any relevant constraints.

Context Window – The amount of text an AI can consider at one time. Larger context windows allow AI to reference more information when generating responses.

D

Deep Learning – A type of machine learning that uses neural networks with many layers to learn complex patterns. Most modern AI language systems are built on deep learning.

Digital Twin – A virtual representation of a real-world entity—such as a person, process, or system—built from data. In personal productivity, a digital twin might be a personal knowledge base that captures and organizes your conversations, writing, and ideas for later retrieval.

E

Ethics Framework – A structured approach to making moral decisions. Common frameworks include consequentialism (judging by outcomes), deontology (judging by duties and rules), and virtue ethics (judging by character). In this book, we argue that frameworks are useful but insufficient without deeper values to guide them.

F

Fine-tuning – Adjusting a pre-trained AI model for specific tasks or domains by training it further on specialized data.

Flourishing – A vision of human life that goes beyond mere survival or productivity to include meaning, purpose, deep relationships, growth, and connection to something larger than oneself. In this book, human flourishing is the ultimate goal that AI should serve.

G

Generative AI – AI systems that can create new content—text, images, audio, video—rather than just analyzing existing content. Large language models are a type of generative AI.

Guardrails — Limitations built into AI systems to prevent harmful or inappropriate outputs. Guardrails might prevent AI from generating certain types of content or taking certain actions.

H

Hallucination — When an AI system generates information that seems plausible but is actually false or fabricated. AI hallucinations can include invented facts, fake citations, or confident statements about things the AI doesn't actually know.

Human-in-the-loop — A design approach where humans remain involved in AI processes, reviewing and approving AI outputs before they're used. Ensures human oversight of AI-assisted work.

I

Inference — The process of an AI system generating output based on input. When you ask an AI a question, the generation of the answer is inference.

Input — The information you provide to an AI system—your question, prompt, or the content you want it to process.

L

Large Language Model (LLM) — An AI system trained on vast amounts of text that can generate human-like responses, answer questions, and assist with various language tasks. ChatGPT, Claude, and similar systems are large language models.

M

Machine Learning (ML) – A branch of AI where systems learn patterns from data rather than being explicitly programmed with rules. Most modern AI systems use machine learning.

Model – The AI system itself—the trained neural network that processes input and generates output. "GPT-4" and "Claude" are examples of AI models.

Moral Deflection – The temptation to use technology to avoid responsibility for harm. Examples include claiming "the AI did it" or "the algorithm decided" rather than accepting personal accountability for AI-assisted outcomes.

N

Natural Language Processing (NLP) – AI techniques for understanding and generating human language. LLMs are a type of NLP system.

Neural Network – A computing system loosely modeled on biological brains, consisting of interconnected nodes that process information. Deep neural networks power modern AI systems.

O

Output – The AI's response to your input—the text, answer, or content it generates.

P

Parameters – The numerical values in an AI model that are adjusted during training to improve performance. More parameters generally (but not always) means more capable models.

Pattern Matching – Recognizing similarities between new information and information seen during training. AI excels at pattern matching but can struggle when situations don't match familiar patterns.

Prompt – The instruction or question you give to an AI system to tell it what you want it to do. "Prompting" is the act of crafting these instructions.

Presuppositions – The underlying assumptions and beliefs we bring to any question, often without realizing it. Being honest about our presuppositions, as philosopher Francis Schaeffer argued, is more intellectually rigorous than pretending we start from a neutral position.

Prompt Engineering – The practice of crafting effective prompts to get better results from AI systems. While the term suggests technical precision, effective prompting is more about clear communication than special techniques.

R

RAG (Retrieval-Augmented Generation) – A technique where AI retrieves relevant information from a database before generating a response, helping it access current or specialized information.

S

Shadow AI – The use of unauthorized or unapproved AI tools by employees within an organization. Similar to "shadow IT," shadow AI creates risks when employees use consumer AI tools for work purposes without organizational oversight or governance.

T

Token — A unit of text that AI processes. Tokens might be words, parts of words, or punctuation. AI systems have limits on how many tokens they can process at once.

Training — The process of teaching an AI model to recognize patterns by exposing it to large amounts of data. Training happens before you use the model; your interactions don't typically retrain the model.

Training Data — The information used to train an AI model. The quality and scope of training data significantly affects what the model can do and how well it performs.

Transformer — The neural network architecture underlying most modern large language models. Transformers are particularly good at processing sequential data like text.

V

Verification — The process of checking whether AI-generated information is accurate. Because AI can hallucinate, verification of important claims is essential.

Note: AI terminology evolves rapidly. These definitions reflect common usage as of early 2026.

Resources for Continued Learning

The AI landscape changes rapidly. Specific tools, platforms, and resources that exist today may evolve significantly within months. The resources below were current as of early 2026, but the principles in this book apply regardless of which specific tools you use.

Books for Deeper Understanding

Related Books by the Author

Agentic Development: The Complete Guide to AI-Assisted Coding (3rd Edition) The technical companion to this book, written for software developers and technical professionals. Covers AI-assisted coding workflows, context management, and building with AI tools. Available on Amazon in Kindle, paperback, and hardcover.

The 75% Secret: A Definitive Guide to the Hidden Job Market Practical strategies for career transitions and job searching in an AI-influenced market. Available on Amazon.

Recommended Reading on AI and Technology

Ethan Mollick, *Co-Intelligence: Living and Working with AI* (2024) — A Wharton professor's practical guide to working alongside AI. Mollick brings research rigor with accessible writing, making it an excellent companion to this book's approach.

Kevin Roose, *Futureproof: 9 Rules for Humans in the Age of Automation* (2021) — Practical career advice for staying relevant as AI capabilities expand. Roose is a New York Times technology columnist who writes with clarity and nuance.

Kai-Fu Lee, *AI Superpowers* (2018) and *AI 2041* (2021) — Lee, a former head of Google China, offers both a geopolitical perspective on AI development and, in the later book, accessible fiction that illustrates how AI may reshape daily life.

Mustafa Suleyman, *The Coming Wave* (2023) — The co-founder of DeepMind examines the broader implications of AI and biotechnology. Particularly strong on governance and containment challenges.

Brian Christian, *The Alignment Problem* (2020) — A deep but readable exploration of how we ensure AI systems do what we actually want. Essential background for the ethics discussions in Part 5.

On Human Flourishing and Technology

- **C.S. Lewis, *The Abolition of Man*** — A concise, powerful argument for objective moral value, referenced in Chapter 15. Short enough to read in an afternoon; important enough to reread annually.
- **Timothy Keller, *Counterfeit Gods*** — On the danger of making good things into ultimate things, including technology and productivity.
- **Francis Schaeffer, *The God Who Is There* and *He Is There and He Is Not Silent*** — On presuppositions and how

they shape our approach to truth and ethics. Referenced in Chapter 15.

- **Andy Crouch, *The Tech-Wise Family*** – Practical wisdom on maintaining human connection and intentionality in a technology-saturated world.
- **Cal Newport, *Deep Work*** – Not specifically about AI, but essential reading on protecting focused human thinking in an age of technological distraction.

Online Resources

The Author's Work

Synthetic Insights – synthetic-insights.ai The author's organization, focused on practical AI guidance and ethical AI development. Includes companion resources for this book.

Ethics Framework – synthetic-insights.ai/ethics The ethical principles underlying this work, including the philosophical foundations and practical commitments discussed in Part 5.

AI Tools to Explore

The specific tools change frequently. Focus on developing skill with AI assistants in general rather than mastery of any single tool.

General-Purpose AI Assistants - **ChatGPT** (chatgpt.com) – OpenAI's conversational AI. Strong general-purpose capabilities with both free and paid tiers. - **Claude** (claude.ai) – Anthropic's AI assistant. Known for nuanced reasoning and longer-form work. The tool I use most in my own work. - **Gemini** (gemini.google.com) – Google's AI assistant, deeply integrated with Google Workspace. - **Copilot** (copilot.microsoft.com) – Microsoft's AI assistant, integrated with Microsoft 365.

Specialized Tools - **Perplexity** (perplexity.ai) — AI-powered research and search with source citations. - **Grammarly** — AI writing assistance with tone and style guidance. - **Notion AI** — AI capabilities within project management and note-taking. - **Otter.ai** — AI meeting transcription and summarization.

When evaluating any AI tool: - Understand its privacy and data policies before sharing sensitive information - Know its limitations, not just its capabilities - Start with lower-stakes applications before high-stakes ones - Develop your own verification practices (see Chapter 4)

Newsletters and Podcasts

Newsletters - **The Batch** (deeplearning.ai/the-batch) — Andrew Ng's weekly AI newsletter. Concise, credible, and accessible to non-technical readers. - **Stratechery** (stratechery.com) — Ben Thompson's analysis of technology strategy. Paid, but consistently insightful on how AI affects business. - **One Useful Thing** (oneusefulthing.org) — Ethan Mollick's Substack on practical AI use. Directly applicable to the themes in this book.

Podcasts - **Hard Fork** (New York Times) — Kevin Roose and Casey Newton discuss technology news with nuance and humor. - **Practical AI** (changelog.com/practicalai) — Focused on making AI practical and accessible.

Organizational Resources

For those responsible for AI in organizations:

Governance Frameworks - **NIST AI Risk Management Framework** (nist.gov/itl/ai-risk-management-framework) — The most comprehensive US government framework for managing AI risks. Free, well-structured, and regularly updated. - **ISO/IEC 42001:2023** — International standard for AI management systems.

Useful for organizations seeking formal AI governance certification. - **OECD AI Principles** (oecd.ai) — International guidelines adopted by over 40 countries. Good starting point for understanding global AI governance expectations. - **EU AI Act** — The world's first comprehensive AI regulation. Even if you don't operate in Europe, understanding its risk-based approach helps frame organizational AI governance.

Policy Development - Sample AI use policies from leading organizations (search "[your industry] AI acceptable use policy") - Data protection frameworks: GDPR, CCPA/CPRA, HIPAA (for healthcare) - NIST Cybersecurity Framework — Relevant because AI systems introduce new security considerations

Training and Development - **Google AI Essentials** (coursera.org) — Free foundational course suitable for all employees - **LinkedIn Learning AI courses** — Broad selection ranging from executive overview to hands-on practice - **Coursera and edX** — University-backed courses on AI fundamentals, ethics, and applications

---

Building AI Fluency

Practice Deliberately

The best way to develop AI fluency is regular, thoughtful practice:

1. **Start with real tasks.** Use AI for actual work, not just experiments.
2. **Vary your approaches.** Try different ways of accomplishing similar tasks.
3. **Review what works.** Notice which interactions produce good results.
4. **Learn from friction.** When AI struggles, analyze why.
5. **Stay current.** AI capabilities change; your practices should evolve.

Learn from Others

- Follow practitioners who share their AI experiences (not just influencers selling courses)
- Participate in professional communities exploring AI use in your field
- Share your own learning with colleagues—teaching is the best way to solidify understanding

---

Staying Current

Given how quickly AI evolves, staying informed matters:

Be Selective - Not all AI news is worth your attention - Focus on developments that affect your actual use - Ignore most predictions about AI's future—they're usually wrong

Read Primary Sources - AI company announcements and documentation (not just news coverage) - Research papers (even just abstracts and summaries) - Reports from credible organizations (Pew Research, Brookings, McKinsey Global Institute)

Be Skeptical - Both hype and doom are often exaggerated - Claims about AI capabilities deserve verification - Anyone who sounds certain about AI's five-year trajectory is guessing

Focus on Principles - Tools change; principles endure - What you learn about effective AI interaction transfers across tools - Ethical reasoning applies regardless of specific technology

---

A Note on Currency

This resource list will become outdated. AI tools launch and evolve monthly. Websites change. Organizations pivot.

What won't become outdated: - The importance of understanding AI honestly - The value of thoughtful, ethical practice - The principles of effective human-AI interaction - The deeper questions about values and flourishing

Use these resources as starting points, not definitive guides. The best resource for learning AI is your own thoughtful practice.

Resources current as of January 2026

Discussion Questions

These questions are designed for group discussion. They work well for book clubs, workplace learning groups, or study circles exploring AI together.

Part 1: Understanding AI

1. Before reading this book, what was your mental model of AI? How has it changed?
2. Where on the autonomy spectrum are you most comfortable working with AI? Why?
3. What surprised you most about how AI actually works?

Part 2: The Agentic Approach

4. How might the "AI as partner" mindset change how you approach your work?
5. What context do you take for granted that AI would need explicitly stated?
6. Share an example of a communication breakdown with an AI tool. What could have been different?

Part 3: AI in Practice

7. Which practical application of AI is most relevant to your work or life?
8. What tasks would you want to keep distinctly human, even if AI could help?
9. How might AI change your approach to learning new skills?

Part 4: Implications

10. What workforce changes concern you most? What excites you?
11. How should your organization approach AI adoption?
12. What skills do you want to develop to thrive in an AI-augmented world?

Part 5: Ethics and Human Flourishing

13. Where do standard ethics frameworks fall short in guiding AI use?
14. Have you ever used AI in a way that felt ethically uncomfortable afterward? What would you do differently?
15. What role should deeper value traditions play in how we approach technology?
16. The book argues that human dignity is "inherent, not derived from capability." What are the practical implications of that claim for AI development?
17. What does "living well with AI" look like for you personally? What boundaries have you set or do you need to set?

Final Reflection

18. What's one thing you'll do differently after reading this book?
19. What questions do you still have about AI?
20. What did this book get wrong or miss?

Feel free to adapt these questions for your group's interests and context.

About Synthetic Insights Publishing

Synthetic Insights is an independent publishing and advisory firm that produces practical, research-driven guides for business leaders navigating complex challenges. Founded by Brian R. Miller, Synthetic Insights combines deep domain expertise with modern analytical capabilities to deliver content that is substantive, actionable, and grounded in real-world experience.

Our Mission

We believe that the most valuable business knowledge is practical — drawn from direct experience, tested in realistic scenarios, and presented in frameworks that leaders can apply immediately. Every Synthetic Insights publication follows this principle: concept, framework, application.

Our Publications

- **The Activist Investor Campaign: A Board and Executive Survival Guide** — The complete guide to understanding, preparing for, and navigating activist investor campaigns from both sides of the table.

- **Agentic Development: The Complete Guide to AI-Assisted Coding** — The definitive framework for integrating AI tools into professional software development workflows.
- **The 75% Secret** — A definitive guide to the hidden job market and landing your next role.
- **The Dreamer Premium** — A practical, non-technical guide to thinking, working, and thriving in the age of artificial intelligence.
- **The Board Director's Operating Manual** — The essential field guide for new and aspiring board directors navigating their first years of corporate governance.

Our Approach

Synthetic Insights publications are distinguished by:

- **Insider perspectives** — Direct insights from practitioners, not secondhand analysis
- **Practical frameworks** — Step-by-step playbooks that leaders can implement immediately
- **Real-world grounding** — Case studies, simulations, and examples drawn from actual experience
- **Both sides of the table** — Understanding every stakeholder's perspective, not just one

Contact

- **Website:** synthetic-insights.ai
- **Email:** brian@synthetic-insights.ai

Synthetic Insights Publishing — Practical intelligence for business leaders.

www.ingramcontent.com/pod-product-compliance
Lightning Source LLC
LaVergne TN
LVHW010649110826
845149LV00014B/3008

* 9 7 9 8 9 9 4 6 7 3 7 6 8 *